D0163434

Post-tenure Faculty Evaluation:
Threat or Opportunity?

by Christine M. Licata

ASHE-ERIC Higher Education Report No. 1, 1986

Prepared by

Clearinghouse on Higher Education
The George Washington University

Published by

Association for the Study of Higher Education

Jonathan D. Fife,
Series Editor

Cite as
Licata, Christine M. *Post-tenure Faculty Evaluation: Threat or Opportunity?* ASHE-ERIC Higher Education Report No. 1. Washington, D.C.: Association for the Study of Higher Education, 1986.

Cover design by Michael David Brown, Inc., Rockville, Maryland.

The ERIC Clearinghouse on Higher Education invites individuals to submit proposals for writing monographs for the Higher Education Report series. Proposals must include:

1. A detailed manuscript proposal of not more than five pages.
2. A 75-word summary to be used by several review committees for the initial screening and rating of each proposal.
3. A vita.
4. A writing sample.

Library of Congress Catalog Card Number 86-70827
ISSN 0884-0040
ISBN 0-913317-28-4

ERIC® Clearinghouse on Higher Education
The George Washington University
One Dupont Circle, Suite 630
Washington, D.C. 20036

ASHE **Association for the Study of Higher Education**
One Dupont Circle, Suite 630
Washington, D.C. 20036

This publication was partially prepared with funding from the Office of Educational Research and Improvement, U.S. Department of Education under contract no. 400-86-0017. The opinions expressed in this report do not necessarily reflect the positions or policies of OERI or the Department.

EXECUTIVE SUMMARY

Evaluation of faculty performance and assessment of faculty vitality are processes critical to institutional livelihood and renewal. As the higher education community approaches the next decade, greater attention to faculty evaluation can be expected, and there is reason to believe that this attention will not only be directed to an examination of faculty evaluation practices before tenure but will also encompass the evaluation of faculty performance and vitality following tenure—that is, post-tenure evaluation.

The degree of interest and amount of resources applied to these processes have ebbed and flowed over time, tempered by the environmental factors that surround institutions of higher education. The National Commission on Higher Education Issues (1982) recently identified post-tenure evaluation as one of the most pressing issues facing higher education in the next decade. In its summary report, the commission strongly urged that "campus academic administrators working closely with appropriate faculty committees should develop a system of post-tenure evaluation" (p. 10). It also suggested that "nothing will undermine the tenure system more completely than its being regarded as a system to protect faculty members from evaluation" (p. 10) and recommended that a system of post-tenure evaluation be developed on campuses to help ensure faculty competence and strengthen institutional quality (p. 10).

Not all factions in the higher education community support this notion or see the necessity for establishment of such a system, however. Participants at the 1983 Wingspread Conference, Committee A of the AAUP on Academic Freedom and Tenure, and other scholars in the field voice serious reservations about institutions' developing formalized procedures for review of tenured faculty. They believe that sufficient evaluation already occurs and that additional periodic institutional evaluation of tenured faculty would reap little benefit, would be very costly, not only in money and time but also in the diminution of creativity and collegiality, and would ultimately threaten academic freedom.

Clearly, discourse on this topic engenders some very disparate views.

What Factors Influence Current Attention to Post-tenure Evaluation?

Educational planners characterize the next decade in higher education as one wrought with budgetary restraint, steady-state reallocations, declining enrollments, and overall problems of retrenchment. Of equal concern are the predictions that by the late 1980s, approximately 80 percent of faculty will be tenured at institutions where a tenure system operates and that by 2000, the modal age of tenured faculty will be between 55 and 65. These factors are further compounded by the fact that the absence of job mobility and the shortened span of the career ladder have conspired to produce a feeling among some faculty of being "stuck."

In the past, efforts to foster institutional flexibility focused on alternatives or modifications to the traditional tenure system. No conclusive evidence exists, however, to show that tenure adversely affects faculty productivity or teaching effectiveness. Likewise, no substantial evidence suggests that either the abrogation of tenure or the various modifications to tenure schemes are superior to a tenure system (Chait and Ford 1982). The question then becomes, "Can institutions committed to a tenure system yet faced with an uncertain fiscal future reconcile their need to establish some degree of flexibility with the equally critical need to maintain the quality and vitality of the institution and the faculty?" It is precisely in this context that discussion about post-tenure evaluation emerges.

Is Post-tenure Evaluation Compatible with the Principle of Tenure?

Post-tenure evaluation is not in opposition to the principle of tenure and to AAUP policy statements about tenure, provided that the evaluation is not used as grounds for dismissal and that any recommended dismissal is subject to normal academic due process. The AAUP/AAC Commission on Academic Tenure in 1973 recommended that post-tenure evaluation could improve the operation of tenure. Some commentators studying this question also suggest that post-tenure evaluation can strengthen rather than diminish the value of tenure (Bennett and Chater 1984; Chait and Ford 1982; Olswang and Fantel 1980–81).

Do Observers Agree about the Purpose and Value of Post-tenure Evaluation?

The strongest support for post-tenure evaluation is voiced by those who view it as a formative way to reinforce faculty growth and to improve instruction (Bennett and Chater 1984; Zuckert and Friedhoff 1980). Some proponents also suggest its usefulness in decisions about merit pay, promotion, and dismissal for cause.

Apprehension and skepticism about the development of a formal institutional system for periodic review are expressed by those who fear that such systems are unworkable, will undermine the tenure principle by allowing for termination of tenured faculty, will devalue rigorous pre-tenure evaluation, and will erode collegial relationships (AAUP 1983).

What Conclusions and Recommendations Emerge from This Study of Post-tenure Evaluation?

Institutions interested in developing a process for post-tenure review should carefully investigate the potential advantages and disadvantages that such a system might eventuate. Institutional type, climate, and mission are intervening variables that may affect the advisability and feasibility of establishing such a process. For institutions wishing to pursue this notion further, the following considerations should be thoroughly examined before design and implementation of a process for post-tenure review:

1. The purpose of the evaluation should be clearly articulated, and all other aspects of the evaluation plan should tie directly to the established purpose. Institutions must decide whether the evaluation will be formative or summative in purpose.
2. Faculty must be involved in the design of the plan, and commitment by the administration must be evident.
3. Faculty and administrators should agree on the specifics of the plan. Particular attention should be given to the need for multiple sources of input, identified areas and criteria for assessment, and agreement on standards for assessment.
4. Flexibility and individualization should be emphasized in the plan and in the criteria used for evalua-

tion. Evaluation schemes must respond to the transitional stages in an academic's life while at the same time recognizing institutional priorities.

5. Strong evidence supports the link between faculty development and rewards and post-tenure evaluation. Such a link is critical in a formative evaluation scheme.
6. Innovative approaches to planning and evaluation are needed. The concept of growth contracts deserves renewed attention.

Basic to each of these considerations is the need for expanded research on the status, the practices, and the effectiveness of current post-tenure evaluation plans.

ADVISORY BOARD

CONSULTING EDITORS

L. Jackson Newell
Professor and Dean
University of Utah

Steven G. Olswang
Assistant Provost for Academic Affairs
University of Washington

Harold Orlans
Office of Programs and Policy
United States Civil Rights Commission

Patricia Rueckel
Executive Director
National Association for Women Deans, Administrators, and Counselors

Charles B. Saunders, Jr.
Vice President for Government Relations
American Council on Education

Richard F. Stevens
Executive Director
National Association of Student Personnel Administrators

James H. Werntz, Jr.
Vice Chancellor for Academic Affairs
University of North Carolina

CONTENTS

FOREWORD

The facts are not new concerning the issue of post-tenure evaluation. It is well-known that many if not most higher education institutions have reached a saturation point with tenured positions. Since the professoriate is only middle-aged (average age is late 40s), faculty have perhaps 20 more years of service. The issue can be framed thusly: under the current tenure system, do we already have procedures that insure accountability and continued productivity? If not, does higher education need to develop evaluation procedures that will guarantee the long-range quality of the system? Is our unshakeable belief in academic freedom making us blind to the need for individual accountability to produce? In blunter terms, will the quality of higher education be sacrificed at the altar of academic freedom?

Academic freedom is an accepted and justified part of collegiate values; raising the specter of post-tenure review should not attack this value. However, colleges and universities have an entrenched faculty whose performance should be accountable and productive. The current tenure system may already provide sufficient procedures for insuring acceptable performance levels. If it does not, we must institute a system that not only protects job security and promotes academic freedom but that also insures continued high productivity. In other words, discussions of post-tenure evaluation must include recognition of the many benefits of the tenure system, which does provide job security while maintaining academic freedom.

In this scholarly review of a volatile subject, Christine Licata, assistant dean and director at the School of Business Careers at the National Institute for the Deaf at Rochester Institute of Technology, explores the benefits and pitfalls of post-tenure review. Beginning with an overview of the philosophical arguments for instituting such a treatment, she identifies the major issues of concern and then carefully weighs the evidence to see which procedure can provide quality control while considering job security and academic freedom. This monograph frames the issues so that all parties concerned—administrators, faculty, and trustees—can examine the issue and draw their own conclusions. The health and vitality of the professoriate is becoming one of the dominant issues facing higher education professionals over the next decade. Post-tenure review may well become a central consideration to this issue.

Jonathan D. Fife
Series Editor
Professor and Director
ERIC Clearinghouse on Higher Education
The George Washington University

ACKNOWLEDGMENTS

The author wishes to thank Dr. Joseph A. Greenberg and Dr. Edmund J. Gleazer, Jr., from the George Washington University for their encouragement to pursue this area of research; Dr. Robert McKinney for his helpful guidance; and Dr. Jonathan D. Fife from the ERIC Clearinghouse on Higher Education for his patience and support of this monograph. Special appreciation also goes to Laura Rogers for her technical assistance in processing this manuscript and to Dr. Angelo A. Licata for his abiding understanding and confidence in this total endeavor.

SETTING THE STAGE: Factors Influencing the Focus on Post-tenure Evaluation

Evaluation of faculty performance and assessment of faculty vitality are processes critical to institutional livelihood and renewal. The degree of interest and amount of resources applied to those processes have ebbed and flowed over time, tempered by the environmental factors that surround institutions of higher education (Kirschling 1978).

As the higher education community approaches the next decade, much greater attention to faculty evaluation can be expected, and there is reason to believe that this attention will not only be directed to an examination of faculty evaluation practices before tenure but will also encompass the evaluation of faculty performance and vitality following tenure—that is, post-tenure evaluation.

The National Commission on Higher Education Issues (1982) recently moved post-tenure evaluation into the fore when it identified it as one of the most pressing issues facing higher education. In its summary report, the commission strongly affirmed the importance of tenure as a means to protect academic freedom but at the same time urged that "campus academic administrators, working closely with appropriate faculty committees, should develop a system of post-tenure evaluation" (p. 10). The commission suggested that "nothing will undermine the tenure system more completely than its being regarded as a system to protect faculty members from evaluation" (p. 10) and recommended that a system of peer review be developed on campuses to help ensure faculty competence and strengthen institutional quality (p. 10).

The National Commission on Higher Education Issues (1982) recently . . . identified post-tenure evaluation as one of the most pressing issues facing higher education.

Not all factions in the higher education community endorse this notion or see the necessity for the establishment of such a system, however. Some believe that such periodic, formal institutional evaluation is unnecessary because mechanisms are already in place on campuses that adequately assess performance, particularly as it affects promotion, salary increments, and other types of faculty rewards. And others are concerned that such a system would threaten academic freedom and the tenure principle, abate collegiality, and produce too little overall benefit.

On the other hand, some support the commission's recommendations, viewing post-tenure evaluation as a vehicle to augment the quality and vitality of faculty and believing that most evaluation mechanisms currently in place are informal and unsystematic and therefore not geared to assisting the professional development of faculty.

Clearly, discourse on this topic engenders some very disparate views. The purposes of this report are to explore and analyze the factors that have led to this burgeoning attention to post-tenure evaluation, to review the definition and limitations connected with tenure in general, to identify present practices of post-tenure evaluation, to examine positions of advocacy and of opposition to post-tenure evaluation, and to advance practical considerations that institutions might ponder before modifying or implementing a formal post-tenure evaluation process.

The Higher Education Environment

Many educational planners and prognosticators characterize the next decade in higher education as one earmarked by upheaval and uncertainty and plagued with problems of retrenchment (Mingle and associates 1981) and steady-state reallocation (Eddy 1981). Alarming reports forecast a decline in college enrollments of between 5 and 15 percent over the next 20 years, accompanied by spiraling operational costs and decreased funding (Carnegie Council 1980). Cries for accountability echo forth from trustees, legislators, and the general public (Greene 1976; Moore 1980; Olswang and Lee 1984; Tucker and Mautz 1982).

Some believe that survival depends on an institution's ability to respond flexibly to these changing conditions (Cartter 1975; Cyert 1980; Furniss 1978). Flexibility in highly labor-intensive organizations is difficult, however, particularly in higher education, where it is estimated that faculty and related staff salaries and fringe benefits account for about 70 to 80 percent of most operating budgets (Mortimer and Tierney 1979, p. 35). One reason that such salary expenses are not fluid is that tenure is firmly embedded at many institutions. Approximately 85 percent of all full-time faculty in the United States teach in institutions where a tenure system operates (Chait and Ford 1982, p. 10). Approximately 59 percent of those faculty held tenure in 1981 (Chait and Ford 1982, p. 10), and the percentage presently hovers around 69.5 percent (Carnegie Foundation 1985). Other research indicates that the modal age of tenured faculty is 46 and that such faculty will remain with the same institution for the next two to three decades, thus raising the modal age to somewhere between 55 and 65 by 2000 (Chait and Ford 1982, p. 8; Kerr 1980). Tenured faculty have not been replenished and have become a "stable, static group with less opportunity to move from one institution to another" (Novotny 1981, p. 7). Net faculty additions at institutions hover at about 0 percent (Carnegie Council 1980, p. 305), and faculty movement from one institution to another has dropped from about 8 percent in the mid-1960s to about 1 percent currently (Chait and Ford 1982, p. 7). Almost 30 percent of the faculty in one study admitted to feeling trapped in their jobs because of little opportunity for advancement (Carnegie Foundation 1985).

The Age Discrimination in Employment Act and Amendments of 1978

The graying professoriate and its limited mobility have been further exacerbated by the recent amendments to the Age Discrimination in Employment Act (ADEA). The 1978 amendments to the act extended the mandatory minimum retirement age to 70 but included an exception for higher education institutions until 1982 (Novotny 1981). A post-ADEA survey indicated that most higher education institutions feel that faculty turnover will be very limited in the future as faculty remain in their positions until retirement and few new positions are added (Corwin and Knepper 1978). Because senior faculty generally receive higher salaries than junior faculty, institutions can expect to be faced with constantly increasing salary expenses (Corwin and Knepper 1978). A faculty member who is tenured around the age of 35 and retires at the age of 70 costs an institution approximately $800,000 over the life of his or her tenure (Chait 1980).

Moreover, further alterations in the mandatory retirement age are possible. Several bills are presently under congressional consideration to eliminate the mandatory retirement age from ADEA, and one of them would reinstate the exemption for tenured professors.

While administrators tend to view these environmental and legislative forces as obstructive to institutional flexibility, faculty members tend to see them as erosive to their working conditions (Baldwin 1982). The absence of job mobility and the shortened career ladder have conspired to produce a feeling among some faculty of being "stuck" and without leverage (Kanter 1979; Schuster and Bowen 1985). For some academics, a pall of gloom is produced when this lack of career opportunity and declining standard of living are contrasted against original career expectations (Shulman 1979). The term "demoralized profession" describes this condition (Baldwin et al. 1981), meaning that a dissonance is created when faculty enter teaching with great expectations but ultimately face a constricted future because of such economic and demographic trends. Furthermore, a decrease in extrinsic rewards and an increase in job demands cause a tension in the academic marketplace that threatens the traditionally "strong intrinsic motivation characteristic of college faculty" (Austin and Gamson 1983, p. 44). Approximately 40 percent of the faculty in one study reported themselves to be less enthusiastic now about their careers than when they started, and over half indicated they would accept a position outside of academia if one were available (Carnegie Foundation 1985).

If one is to believe, as so many have for so long, that the faculty are the university, then the quality of their work life is extremely important; "the most important thing about a college is the quality of the lives of the people who staff it" (Bailey 1974, p. 27). Administrators and faculty hold equally important and often diverse perspectives on this issue of flexibility, yet they also share a common purpose that is driven by a desire to maintain a vibrant, healthy, and productive institution.

In the face of an aging, immobile faculty, shifting enrollment trends, declining budgets, spiraling costs, and external calls for accountability and self-regulation, what options promote institutional flexibility and foster faculty vitality and renewal?

It is in the context of this question and in light of these intervening variables that a need surfaces within the higher education community to find viable options to counter the forces that threaten faculty and institutional quality and flexibility. The National Commission on Higher Education Issues (1982) positioned its recommendations on tenure and post-tenure review within the larger rhetorical context related to improving the overall quality in higher education and reinforcing the level of public confidence in it. Thus, recent attention on post-tenure evaluation emerges in part as a measure to assuage the potential negative effects that present demographic, legislative, and environmental forces might induce on faculty work life and on institutional vitality. "The use of a periodic performance review system for tenured faculty may, in the long run, provide a needed constructive alternative to other more drastic measures to which institutions have turned to guarantee institutional quality and necessary levels of administrative flexibility" (Olswang and Fantel 1980–81, p. 1).

AN OVERVIEW OF POST-TENURE FACULTY EVALUATION

Systematic evaluation of faculty before tenure has traditionally found strong support in colleges and universities as a vehicle for making appropriate personnel decisions and for effecting improved performance (Centra 1979; Dressel 1976; Miller 1972, 1974; Smith 1976). Discussion of systematic and formal evaluation of faculty after tenure has not received the same kind of attention over the years; it originally surfaced in the literature as a progeny of the proposals to modify tenure. Such proposals have included non-tenure-track appointments, tenure quotas, extended probationary periods, and dissolution of the up-and-out rule.[1] For the most part, however, post-tenure evaluation when viewed in this context is seen primarily as a vehicle to remove tenured faculty on grounds related to unsatisfactory performance.

Post-tenure evaluation is not in opposition to the tenure principle or to policy statements of the American Association of University Professors (AAUP), provided that the "evaluation itself is not grounds for dismissal and any separations recommended are subject to academic due process in the normal manner" (Linney 1979, p. 7).

Post-tenure evaluation is not in opposition to the tenure principle or to policy statements of the American Association of University Professors.

Even the Commission on Academic Tenure (the Keast Commission) (AAUP/AAC 1973) suggested that post-tenure evaluation could improve the operation of tenure and recommended that ". . . each institution develop methods of evaluating the teaching effectiveness of both its nontenured and its tenured faculty and procedures for reflecting these evaluations in pertinent personnel actions" (p. 36).

A review of all the relevant literature on tenure led one commentator to conclude that "nowhere in the literature did any of the proponents of tenure argue for the concept of tenure as lifetime employment or sinecure not subject to review or performance evaluation" (Habecker 1981, p. 60). As post-tenure evaluation presumes the existence of an operational tenure system, a brief review of the definition and limitations of tenure serves as helpful background to a discussion of post-tenure evaluation.

Tenure: Definition and Limitations

The historical and philosophical grounds for tenure have remained essentially unchanged over the years. Basically,

1. See, for example, Chait and Ford (1982, pp. 41–141) and Mortimer, Bagshaw, and Masland (1985, pp. 22–38) for a more complete discussion of modifications to the tenure system.

tenure advances academic freedom by offering to the scholar certain protections from external and internal influences that might interfere with free inquiry and with the advancement and dissemination of knowledge (Mix 1978; Walden 1979, 1980). One of the staunchest proponents of tenure points out that tenure is the conduit for academic freedom and as such is critical to the special functioning of the university as a community (Brewster 1972). For institutions to be "alive and productive," colleagues must disagree and dispute. It is academic freedom that spawns the free and unconditional "intellectual comfort" necessary to protect and promote the essence of the university (p. 383). Other advocates assert that tenure is essential to the protection of academic freedom (Habecker 1981; Tucker and Mautz 1982), that it increases institutional stability and loyalty (Walden 1979), that it promotes faculty excellence and rigor (Davidson 1982; Van Alstyne 1978), and that it offsets the poor economic plight of the profession by providing some job security (Chait and Ford 1982).

Conversely, its critics purport that tenure perpetuates mental deterioration, sloth, professional incompetence, and the abandonment of professional standards among faculty (Nisbet 1973), that it obstructs institutional change and innovation (Walden 1979), that it limits faculty mobility, career growth, and collegiality (O'Toole 1978), and that it destroys academic freedom and encourages sinecure (Silber 1973).

Some of the scholars engaged in this debate have pointed out that the principle of tenure is not the culprit but that the individual interpretation and application of it is (Davidson 1982; Lang 1975; Smith 1974; Tucker and Mautz 1982; Walden 1980). The Keast Commission also underscored this notion:

> *The problems with which tenure is clearly implicated arise not from anything in the principle of tenure itself but from deficiencies in the operation of the tenure system in individual institutions. The Commission believes that a strong commitment to making tenure work, combined with measures to improve its operation in different institutional settings, can reduce many of the deficiencies* (AAUP/AAC 1973, p. 23).

In this same vein, the National Commission on Higher Education Issues urged institutions "to review and, if needed, revise their procedures . . . to assure themselves and the public that the [pretenure evaluation] procedures will produce fair, rigorous, and relevant evaluations" (1982, p. 9).

Historically, the AAUP has functioned as the guardian of academic freedom and tenure. In that role, it has issued several policy statements that offer guidance to the academic community, and many campuses have readily adopted and integrated AAUP documents into their institutional policy. In particular, the 1940 Statement of Principles on Academic Freedom and Tenure and the 1957 Recommended Institutional Regulations on Academic Freedom and Tenure are two such guiding documents. The 1940 statement, jointly and largely written in conjunction with the Association of American Colleges (AAC) and endorsed by more than 100 learned societies, states:

> *Tenure is a means to certain ends—specifically (1) freedom of teaching and research and of extramural activities and (2) a sufficient degree of economic security to make the profession attractive to men and women of ability. Freedom and economic security—hence tenure—are indispensible to the success of an institution fulfilling its obligation to its students and to society* (AAUP 1984a, p. 3).

The Commission on Academic Tenure expanded the original definition of tenure:

> *[Tenure is] an arrangement under which faculty appointments in an institution of higher education are continued until retirement for age or physical disability, subject to dismissal for adequate cause or unavoidable termination on account of financial exigency or change of institutional program* (AAUP/AAC 1973, p. 256).

In making these concepts operational, institutions have developed a process that includes a probationary period before the decision to confer tenure is made. If professional excellence and promise have been demonstrated effectively during this probationary period, as judged by peers, tenure is granted. After the award of tenure, any ensuing attempt to dismiss a tenured faculty member requires appropriate due process.

The term "judicialized tenure" has been employed to denote the context of tenure today: Tenure guarantees academic freedom by granting faculty the presumption of continued "fitness" in their position and likewise promises a formal hearing by peers when such "fitness" comes under question (Metzger 1979, p. 8). The courts have made it clear that tenure is not a vested right but represents a presumption of continued employment under normal circumstances (Mix 1978).

Limitations of tenure—dismissal for cause

Tenure systems generally state in a formal way that dismissal of tenured faculty will be for stated and proven cause. The 1940 AAUP statement on academic freedom and tenure and the 1958 Statement of Procedural Standards for Faculty Dismissal do not, however, provide an explicit definition of cause. From an examination of these AAUP statements, of various institutions' policies, and of relevant court cases, five generally accepted categories for cause emerge: "incompetence (mental incompetence as well as incompetence in subject matter areas), immorality or moral turpitude, neglect of duty, violation of institutional rules, and insubordination" (Olswang and Fantel 1980–81, p. 12).

What is clear is that the specific definition of cause is particular to an institution and is an institutional prerogative. Once formulated, however, it is usually stated in institutional policy and procedural guidelines.

Institutional procedures for dismissal for cause and the protections afforded the tenured faculty member are determined and influenced by the specific nature of the institution, that is, whether the institution is public or private. Because tenured faculty employed by public institutions are protected by the Constitution, tenure in this environment provides an expectancy of continued employment. This supposition of continued employment is interpreted as a property right, and termination of this right for cause requires that due process procedures under the Fourteenth Amendment be accorded the individual. The Supreme

Court established a definition of property interest in *Board of Regents* v. *Roth* [408 U.S. 564 (1972)]:

> *To have a property interest in a benefit, a person clearly must have more than an abstract need or desire for it. He must have more than a unilateral expectation of it. He must, instead, have a legitimate claim of entitlement to it. . . . It is a purpose of the constitutional right to a hearing to provide an opportunity for a person to vindicate those claims* (p. 577).

In the past, the courts generally have endeavored to ensure that procedural due process is provided fairly to the tenured faculty member. A formal, issued statement detailing the reasons for termination and an opportunity to respond to such charges are necessary.

> *Courts have upheld the right of colleges to base employment decisions on subjective judgments of quality and performance and have focused their attention on the fairness of the decision-making procedures* (Hendrickson and Lee 1983, p. 13).

On the other hand, faculty in private institutions are not subject to the procedural requirements governing state action in the Constitution. Instead, conditions of faculty employment are determined by contract law, and the procedures to be afforded tenured faculty must be contained in the contract of employment. If the faculty contract does not provide for procedural due process, it is difficult for the terminated faculty member to find recourse through the courts unless it can be proved that the contract was invalid from the onset or was in violation of public policy (Habecker 1981). Frequently, however, AAUP guidelines are included in private institutions' formal tenure policies. In that case, the attendant definition of cause is used.

Statistics are generally unavailable about the yearly numbers of terminations for cause in either public or private institutions. One recent study (Licata 1984) indicated that in nine community colleges, less than 1 percent of post-tenure evaluations occurring over the past five years were considered to be unsatisfactory (p. 133). Of that number, dismissal resulted in only 7 percent of the cases. "To date, few college faculty terminations based on cause have reached reportable stages in litigation'' (Olswang and Fantel 1980–81, p. 12). A need clearly exists for further research that would validate or invalidate the general perception that very few tenured faculty are dismissed for cause.

If the intended institutional purpose for post-tenure evaluation is to remove incompetence, then it becomes a dismissal for cause, and institutions must be guided by appropriate procedures determined largely by institutional type and policy and by legal precedent. Due process is critically important in such instances.

Limitations of tenure—financial exigency

Financial adversity or exigency, usually precipitated by recent downward trends in enrollment, students' interest in certain academic disciplines, and funding, has spawned the dismissal of tenured faculty across the country (Farrell 1982; Scully 1982).

According to the 1973 AAUP/AAC definition of tenure, financial exigency is a legitimate reason for dismissal of tenured faculty, and exigency is defined as ''an imminent financial crisis that threatens the survival of the institution as a whole and that cannot be alleviated by less dramatic means'' (AAUP 1982, p. 23). Moreover, the precise parameters of what constitutes financial exigency vary from institution to institution, with the courts placing the burden of proof on the institution when a dismissed faculty member files for reinstatement (Mix 1978). Further examination of the court's position on financial exigency and its effect on the termination of tenured faculty is important to a discussion of post-tenure evaluation, because if institutions can legally dismiss tenured faculty in a financial emergency, then the question becomes which tenured faculty are dismissed, how it is decided, and whether the results of post-tenure evaluation are used in making that determination.

In *Scheuer* v. *Creighton University* [260 N.W. 2d 595 (1977)], the court ruled that the fiscal status of a department or a college rather than an entire university can constitute exigency. Thus, a definition of operating funds, not the AAUP's definition of survival, has found support in the courts. This development is significant for institutions and faculty, because using this definition of deficient operating funds, the courts have upheld terminations based on bona fide financial exigency in numerous instances.[2]

The courts have upheld that the officers of an institution must make the declaration of financial exigency in good faith and may not use financial exigency as a pretext for the dissolution of tenure.

> *In the several cases that have been brought by tenured faculty members objecting to their removal for budgetary reasons, the courts have consistently held that tenure is subject to termination by the institution if the governing body determines that the financial need for doing so is bona fide [and] made in good faith and the rules of the institution are followed in effecting the terminations* (Olswang 1982–83, p. 436).

The preliminary findings of a recent study disclosed that during 1978 to 1983, 4,000 faculty were laid off in four-year colleges throughout the United States because of financial difficulties. Of the 4,000, 1,200 were tenured (Scully 1983). The particular experiences of 52 tenured faculty laid off at Temple University led one commentator to question the meaning of tenure within the parameters of retrenchment (Heller 1984a). In the case at Temple, 48 of the 52 faculty elected early retirement, severance pay, or another position within the institution. In the case of the remaining four faculty, however, arbitrators ruled that the university had "no obligation to give retrenched faculty members temporary assignments after their layoff notification" (p. 25).

The pervasiveness of collegiate experiences with financial exigency has been difficult to document, and one recent study purported that situations of exigency have not occurred with the frequency that earlier predictions had suggested. The Project on Reallocation in Higher Educa-

2. See, for example, *Levitt* v. *Board of Trustees of Nebraska State College,* 376 F. Supp. 945 (D. Neb. 1974); *Johnson* v. *Board of Regents of the University of Wisconsin System,* 510 F.2d 975 (7th Cir. 1975); *AAUP* v. *Bloomfield College,* 136 N.J. Super. 249, 346 A.2d 615 (1975); *Browzin* v. *Catholic University of America,* 527 F.2d 843 (D.C. Cir. 1975); *Klein* v. *the Board of Higher Education of the City of New York,* 434 F. Supp. 1113 (S.D.N.Y. 1977); *Krotkoff* v. *Goucher College,* 585 F.2d 675 (4th Cir. 1978); *Lumpert* v. *University of Dubuque,* 225 N.W.2d 168 (Iowa Ct. of Appeals 1977); *Scheuer* v. *Creighton University,* 260 N.W.2d 595 (1977).

tion, a national study conducted recently at Pennsylvania State University, collected data on the reallocation, reduction, and prevailing faculty staffing practices at four-year colleges and universities (Mortimer, Bagshaw, and Masland 1985). Of the 318 respondent institutions, about 16 percent indicated that at least one faculty member had been retrenched between 1977 and 1982 (p. 48). (For the purpose of that study, retrenchment was defined as "the dismissal or layoff of tenured faculty members or the dismissal of nontenured faculty members in mid-contract for reasons other than just cause or medical reasons" (pp. 47–48).) A conclusion drawn from these data and other enrollment data for the same institutions led to the hypothesis that managing catastrophic decline was not as much of a reality for those institutions as was managing uncertainty about institutional resources. In any case, these court opinions and college experiences help administrators and faculty recognize the importance of preparation for retrenchment.

The AAUP provides guidelines that help guard against arbitrary and capricious institutional action (Brown 1976). Reaching consensus between the administration and faculty on the appropriate policy and procedures to follow when faculty retrenchment is imminent demands patience and foresight. Developing the policy and procedures before the need for them arises is strongly advised, although not always feasible. In general, the definition and decision that financial exigency exists should if at all possible involve input from faculty; further, the methods and criteria for making faculty cuts, while a responsibility of the administration, should also involve consultation with faculty (Mingle and associates 1981; Mix 1978; Olswang 1982–83). While many institutions use seniority as the basis for determining who is retrenched, the courts have upheld academic competence and institutional need [*Brenna* v. *Southern Colorado State College,* 589 F.2d 475 (10th Cir. 1978); *Bignall* v. *North Idaho College,* 538 F.2d 243 (9th Cir. 1976)].

The courts have upheld the removal of tenured faculty in cases of financial exigency, program discontinuation, or program reductions. The institution must, however, develop specific criteria to be applied in making such determinations, and those criteria must be applied fairly and not used as a means to abrogate tenure or penalize tenured faculty who have exercised their right to academic freedom (Olswang 1982–83, p. 437). At this time, it seems improbable that institutions under financial duress will use the performance of tenured faculty and their viability to specific programmatic needs as indices to be weighed in any decisions about removal.

Purposes of Post-tenure Evaluation

Undergirding and driving any evaluation plan is a preestablished purpose for the evaluation. In the case of post-tenure evaluation, the literature mentions three basic yet not necessarily compatible purposes: (1) to supply documentation for removal for incompetence; (2) to provide input for personnel decisions in the areas of reductions in force, merit raises, and promotions; and (3) to support faculty development and improved instruction.

Removal for incompetence

Some advocates of the need to evaluate tenured faculty with the ultimate sanction of dismissal contend that such a process need not discourage faculty creativity (Linnell 1979; Moore 1980; Nisbet 1973). Historically, dismissal of tenured faculty for cause is rare, but once removal for incompetence becomes more than just a theory, the academic community will tolerate it (Allhouse 1974; Carr 1972).

Post-tenure evaluation has been characterized as a staffing practice that can be used to increase the number of tenured faculty leaving an institution, thereby providing an opportunity for institutions to reduce expenditures, reallocate resources, and reduce committed long-term resources to tenured positions (Mortimer, Bagshaw, and Masland 1985). Yet the reporting institutions in the Project on Reallocation indicated that while over half (about 154) of them had a method for systematically reviewing all tenured faculty, "less than 7 percent . . . reported that negative reviews were used to terminate tenured faculty" (p. 41).

The recently reported embattlement between the faculty and president at Texas Tech University grew out of this very issue. In that institution's proposed tenure policy, post-tenure reviews are required every five years, "with termination possible if performance [is] found to be unsatisfactory" (Heller 1984b, p. 19).

Presently, however, those who envision post-tenure evaluation as a punitive measure, solely as a means to dismiss the incompetent, are in the minority and generally are at odds with various faculty groups, and such a practice not only constitutes a deviation from the traditional norm but also requires that institutions have a systematic way to define and cite what constitutes satisfactory and unsatisfactory performance as well as a mechanism for remediation (Mortimer, Bagshaw, and Masland 1985). Further, the importance of employing appropriate due process in such instances cannot be underplayed. The National Education Association (NEA) and the American Federation of Teachers (AFT) oppose post-tenure reviews that are intended to be used to repeal the award of tenure. These organizations do not oppose it, however, when it is used for faculty development (Perry 1983). The AAUP has not yet registered an official position, but some commentators believe that if such evaluations were employed to terminate tenured faculty for cause without appropriate chance for remediation and due process, the AAUP would denounce the process (Chait and Ford 1982).

> *The apparent reluctance of institutions to use post-tenure review for dismissal on grounds of incompetence underscores the relatively privileged position of the individual tenured faculty member when institutions seek to reduce expenditures or reallocate resources. The general pattern of the Project on Reallocation data suggests that most four-year colleges and universities go to considerable lengths to avoid terminating tenured faculty* (Mortimer, Bagshaw, and Masland 1985, p. 41).

An underlying assumption behind advocacy of post-tenure evaluation for the purpose of dismissing the incompetent is that faculty performance diminishes after tenure. Yet the research related to the effect of tenure and age on teaching effectiveness and productivity does not seem to back up this claim (Creswell 1985).

Effect of tenure on teaching effectiveness. Some adversaries of tenure have placed the blame for ineffective teaching, decreased faculty productivity, and general lack of faculty adaptability on the tenure process itself. This blanket condemnation, however, covers the fact that the culprit is not tenure but "tenure's purported consequences" (Blackburn 1972, p. 3). An examination of the research related to faculty productivity and adaptability reveals no correlation between ineffective classroom teaching and a faculty member's lack of adaptiveness, age, and faculty rank. The older, tenured faculty group, however, did vary more in performance. When the rating for teaching effectiveness given by students in two liberal arts colleges was plotted against age and rank, no correlation existed. Yet faculty who received the highest and the lowest ratings were those in the highest rank and age brackets (Blackburn 1972). The evidence, at least in the early 1970s, did not support any causal relationship between tenure and the charges leveled against it related to declines in effective teaching.

Faculty themselves believe that tenure has no significant effect, positive or negative, on the effectiveness of teaching (Eble 1971). Moreover, the lack of administrative initiative to replace incompetent tenured faculty is related more to matters of time than to tenure. The investment of time required to build and document a case of classroom incompetence and its political ramifications generally prohibit administrators from doing so, given the other demands on their professional lives. Thus, time, not tenure, is the culprit (Eble 1973).

Faculty themselves believe that tenure has no significant effect, positive or negative, on the effectiveness of teaching.

Other researchers have looked more recently at this same issue and concluded that tenure is not the determining factor in measuring the effectiveness of teaching (Habecker 1981). Most research studies show no difference in effective teaching when viewed against variables like faculty rank and tenure status, or if a difference in effectiveness is noted, it is positively skewed toward higher ranks and among tenured faculty (Habecker 1981). Associate professors and full professors (more than five years from retirement) are more comfortable with teaching and rate their teaching skills and rapport with students more highly than do junior faculty (Baldwin and Blackburn 1981). "Student ratings are lower for teachers in their first year or two of teaching but relatively unrelated to age after that" (McKeachie 1983, p. 60).

Effect of tenure on faculty productivity. A solid and conclusive base of systematic research on the effects of tenure on faculty scholarly productivity does not exist. One researcher contrasted the percentage increase in the number of tenured faculty during 1969 to 1975 with the percentage decrease in the number of faculty who reported zero publications over that same time span, concluding that insofar as publications are an indication of productivity, no decrease in productivity could be noted (Trow 1977).

Another researcher tested the premise that productivity declines after tenure by analyzing four measures of productivity (teaching, research, professional service, and community service) against favorable or unfavorable attitudes toward faculty tenure and by asking tenured respondents to judge their own productivity following tenure. A tenure attitude scale was used to analyze faculty responses to the question of whether the productivity of persons they knew increased or decreased after tenure was awarded. About 95 percent of the tenured faculty respondents stated that tenure made no difference in their level of productivity or that productivity had actually increased since tenure was awarded (Walden 1979, p. 155).

Other research confirms these findings. Based on a definition of productivity as the number of articles appearing in a referred journal over a one-year period, one study was unable to discern any significant differences between the productivity level of tenured and untenured faculty who were matched according to age, seniority, discipline, and degree (Orpen 1982). Furthermore, the productivity level of faculty after tenure was only slightly higher than it had been before tenure.

Another study examined the relationship between age and one selected measure of productivity—research and professional activity. The researchers concluded that "career age (and possibly tenure status) is a poor predictor of research–professional activity" (Bayer and Dutton 1977, p. 279). In addition, a corollary finding indicated that the results in terms of productivity for one academic discipline did not apply to another. Thus, during steady-state staffing, it is not possible to establish a "standard educational policy applicable to all members of an age cohort" (p. 279).

In sum, the available research does not support the notion that either effective teaching or scholarly productivity declines after tenure is awarded or is related in any way to age (Lawrence 1984).

Personnel matters

Reductions in force. The posture of the courts in upholding dismissal of tenured faculty by institutions faced with financial exigency has prompted some institutions to involve faculty and administrators in the development of the criteria to be used in reductions in force (RIFs) (Lombardi 1974; Melchiori 1982; Mingle and associates 1981). The question of whether faculty performance can be used as a factor in determining whether tenured faculty are retrenched has received very limited attention. Generally, such deliberations have not urged institutions to use the performance of tenured faculty as a factor in those decisions. Only one institution could be found—Miami-Dade Community College—that reported "consideration" of tenured faculty's effective performance as a possible deciding criterion to be used in such a process (Zaharis 1973). "When the need for RIF loomed, many administrators felt it would allow them to strengthen the faculty by eliminating weak instructors. With the rare exception, [it] has not happened" (Lombardi 1974, p. 56).

The question then becomes, "Do you retain the 'best' faculty in the institution to staff the programs or do you narrow that choice by first concentrating on the untenured faculty for removal?" (Olswang 1982–83, p. 439). The reasons advanced in favor of using performance and institutional need rather than tenure status or seniority revolve around several factors. First, in today's market the credentials of both tenured and nontenured faculty are generally fairly comparable. Second, the currency of knowledge possessed by nontenured faculty may in fact be more important to programs than the depth of knowledge possessed by tenured faculty. Third, the likelihood that some nontenured faculty will not be granted tenure because of substandard performance while some tenured faculty continue in the ranks despite substandard performance helps spur the notion that the best may not always appear in the tenured ranks. This rationale is countered, however, by the realization that the use of criteria based on performance and need may adversely affect faculty morale and engender a fear that tenure is meaningless. Whether this situation in turn can act as a disincentive in attracting new faculty is another concern. On the other hand, the opinion that faculty may view an emphasis on performance and need as positive signals that accountability and institutional health are key institutional values leading to institutional stability is also worthy of consideration (Olswang 1982–83).

Whether institutions will attempt to look at performance and viability in relationship to programmatic needs as factors to be weighed in decisions to retain faculty is not clear but highly unlikely at this time. Should some institutions decide to do so, then summative post-tenure evaluation or some other measurement scheme becomes a crucial necessity.

Merit pay. A national focus on excellence in teaching and the concomitant desire for accountability are two primary reasons for the recent resurgence in discussions about merit pay (McMillen 1984). Some view the provision of a basis for making decisions related to rewards for meritorious performance as a legitimate purpose for post-tenure evaluation (Bennett and Chater 1984). Others are concerned that the tenure system does not address the various stages of development in a faculty member's life, insisting that most tenure plans offer no rewards or incentives for faculty growth (Brookes and German 1983).

Such a lockstep, rewardless system should be altered, and one way to do so is to base faculty salaries solely on performance (Hellweg and Churchman 1981). Practically speaking, however, commentators are far from unanimous on the feasibility and appropriateness of merit raises. Although merit pay would provide incentives for accomplishment, such a plan necessitates systematic evaluation. Further, the idea of monetary rewards negates a faculty member's professional sense of excellence for the sake of excellence. Historically, merit pay has never been a component of the salary structure in highly esteemed professions (Friedman 1984). One attempt to gain an understanding of what merit means to academics resulted in a review of 417 letters written by peers to support merit increases for colleagues. "Teaching was strongly emphasized in 28 percent of the letters and not mentioned in 31 percent, research was strongly emphasized in 52 percent and not mentioned in 27 percent, and administrative service was strongly emphasized in 56 percent and not mentioned in only 18 percent" (Lewis 1984, p. 56), leading to the conclusion that more emphasis is put on administrative tasks than one might expect. More astounding, though, was the fact that although in over 85 percent of the letters where a specific task related to teaching, research, or service was mentioned, "there was rarely any proof that the candidate had performed meritoriously" (p. 56). Coincidentally, it was for this precise reason that a merit system was abandoned at Brookdale Community College in New Jersey: Faculty had difficulty defining excellence in teaching (Smith 1984). Merit systems can have the potential to be more of a hazard than a benefit, particularly if the system is not properly planned and designed and the institution is not organized to put the system in practice. Problems of litigation, divisiveness, and the perpetration of additional bureaucracy can result. To work well, an institution must agree on what constitutes meritorious performance and then design an evaluation system that can provide a mechanism to appraise it (McMillen 1984). Two examples illustrate this point.

Recent negotiations between the California State University system and its faculty union have resulted in a revamping of its merit pay system. A proposal by the university system to allocate all salary increases as merit increases was rejected, primarily because of what faculty called a "patronage system" that allowed each of the 19 campus presidents to decide, in the faculty's view arbitrarily, who received the merit increase. Under the new agreement, all faculty are eligible for a 10 percent pay increase, and a fund of $1.5 million is set aside specifically for merit increases. What is significant in this example is that the recipients of the merit increases will be chosen by faculty committees, not solely by administration. The president of the union sees this solution as "the first contract in higher education enforcing collegiality" (McCurdy 1984, p. 21).

Merit pay is a regential mandate for the university system in Texas, with each campus developing its own procedures for implementation. At the University of Texas at Austin, for example, all faculty receive a 3 percent cost-of-living adjustment, after which the top one-third of the faculty receive merit pay allocations. Faculty themselves decide who receives merit increases, judging each other's accomplishments and ranking each accordingly to produce the top five individuals in each academic unit. Not only is this plan developed by faculty; it also "forces evaluation on faculty after tenure" (Roueche 1984).

Discussion of merit pay in relationship to post-tenure evaluation is certain to persist. Whether the adoption of a merit pay system will become a catalyst in some institutions for developing a system of post-tenure evaluation is unclear at present. The potential for a cause-and-effect relationship certainly exists, and a movement toward merit pay can necessitate the establishment of such a mechanism for evaluation.

Promotions. The majority of institutions with a faculty ranking system have a review process for decisions about promotion. Documentation and evidence of achievement based on criteria for promotion are usually required and are usually reviewed by a peer committee. Because on most campuses promotion is optional after tenure is granted, the review is usually at the initiative of the faculty member.

After promotion to full professor is awarded, this type of performance review, if it occurs at all, tends to be more informal. Thus, some suggest, formal post-tenure evaluation can fill the need to review the performance of faculty not engaged in deliberations about promotion, requests for sabbaticals, and similar processes. The point is that, because promotion to full professor and application for other types of faculty rewards are not expected but are self-initiated, professors not choosing to engage such rewards may never experience this type of peer review.

Professional development

Enabling faculty to refocus professional priorities to better align them with institutional needs is another purpose that post-tenure evaluation can serve (Chait and Ford 1982). Tenure studies conducted in Virginia, Montana, Nevada, and Utah recommend the adoption of some form of periodic review of tenured faculty as a means of improving instruction (Greene 1976; Montana Commission 1974; Scully 1982; University of Utah Commission 1971). Such post-tenure evaluations offer the "least modification to regular tenure procedures with the additional capacity for long-range planning and faculty involvement with the growth and development of the college" (Linney 1979, p. 7).

The majority of faculty and administrators in one survey perceived post-tenure evaluation as a means to help a school or a department be more responsible and viewed post-tenure evaluation and faculty development as closely tied (Bolden 1979). Therefore, when a tenured faculty member received a poor evaluation, the consequences were not dismissal but departmental support for improvement. Similarly, a study of community college evaluation procedures found that faculty and administrators strongly supported post-tenure evaluation for the purpose of providing information to be used for faculty development and improvement (Licata 1984).

A recent study of post-tenure evaluation at the University of Queensland in Australia clearly indicated that "the majority of [academic] staff interviewed favoured regular reviews" (Moses 1985, p. 35). Their reasons were based on the belief that such reviews would result in improved performance and the maintenance of high standards, which would spread from individual faculty to the department and ultimately to the entire university.

Support for Post-tenure Evaluation

It is in this context of faculty tuning rather than pruning that one finds the most concentrated support for post-tenure evaluation.

While traditionally "for all intents and purposes, formal evaluation ends where tenure begins" (Bevan 1980, p. 15), some suggest that in a steady-state environment, an institutional approach to fostering quality and responsiveness must include the reinforcement of personal growth and improvement of instruction through pretenure as well as post-tenure faculty evaluation and development (Bevan 1980; Furniss 1978; Linnell 1979; Zuckert and Friedhoff 1980).

In its summary recommendations, the National Commission on Higher Education Issues suggested the idea that the process of post-tenure evaluation should "assure that the tenured faculty has maintained the appropriate level of competence and is performing at a satisfactory level" (1982, p. 10). The commission suggested further that the responsibility lies with faculty and administration to see that unsatisfactory performance is remedied. Ultimately, "incompetent faculty members must not be protected at the expense of the students or the maintenance of quality" (p. 10).

It is in this context of faculty tuning rather than pruning that one finds the most concentrated support for post-tenure evaluation.

Post-tenure evaluation should be one portion of a complement of activities designed for institutional self-regulation (Bennett and Chater 1984). Faculty vitality is seen as a critical factor in maintaining academic excellence, and post-tenure evaluation therefore serves to enhance faculty vitality, in so doing guaranteeing "academic excellence and institutional accountability and integrity" (p. 41). Institutional greatness depends directly on faculty quality, and meritorious faculty performance is therefore critical (Olswang and Fantel 1980–81). Because tenure is basically a contract, it is also good personnel practice to provide a formal way for parties to such a contract to be able to revalidate the original conditions upon which it was established—namely, demonstration of outstanding teaching, research, and service (Olswang and Fantel 1980–81).

The value of periodic evaluation of tenured faculty lies in the fact that it is good personnel policy, but it should be completely disengaged from the issue of whether tenure continues to be necessary (Shapiro 1983). When the emphasis of the review is on professional development, no link to tenure is really necessary (Moses 1985). Such formative reviews give an institution an opportunity to demonstrate the fact that "institutional expectations of staff and individual career expectations can harmonise" (p. 40); "the very structure of educational institutions should help point out the need for a continuing evaluation system that covers tenured as well as nontenured faculty" (Andrews 1985, p. 80).

Thus, most who champion the cause of post-tenure evaluation do so convinced that post-tenure evaluation should be neither punitive in nature nor connected directly to providing evidence for removal for cause. It should rather help move faculty and institutions closer to their mutual goal of academic quality. The role a formal system of evaluation should play in merit raises or in RIFs is far from resolved.

Legal considerations

Recent analysis has confirmed the legal and administrative compatibility of the tenure principle with post-tenure evaluation, and "no evidence [exists] that tenure and rigorous evaluation are incompatible concepts" (Chait and Ford 1982, p. 181). The courts have never held that "a distinct right of academic freedom" exists; rather they have emphasized the importance to society of free inquiry (Olswang and Fantel 1980–81, p. 3). Furthermore, because tenure does not constitute an unqualified right to continued employment, "it is conditional upon a faculty member's maintenance of competence and compliance with contract obligations and the rules of the institution" (p. 30).

Thus, support can be found for the premise that periodic evaluation, appropriately constructed and implemented, can strengthen rather than weaken tenure (Bennett and Chater 1984; Chait and Ford 1982; Olswang and Fantel 1980–81).

Collective bargaining

Does the presence of a union on a campus affect the viability of a post-tenure evaluation plan? As little is known generally about post-tenure evaluation, even less is known about the relationship of collective bargaining and post-tenure evaluation. What we do know is that under most bargaining statutes, all aspects of an evaluation system and its implementing procedures come under the scope of negotiation (Kleingartner 1984). Thus, administrators in such situations must be guided by the collective bargaining agreement; they cannot unilaterally modify or establish post-tenure evaluation except through interaction with the exclusive bargaining representative or when it is agreed that post-tenure evaluation is outside of the contract (Kleingartner 1984).

An example of a negotiated post-tenure evaluation process in a large university setting is that of the California State University system. In 1983, the university system signed its first collective bargaining agreement, which covered over 19,000 faculty. Approximately 10 percent of the contract was devoted to faculty evaluation, making a distinction between the evaluation procedures for probationary faculty, for tenured faculty considered for promotion, and for tenured faculty not being considered for promotion. Specifically, the contract indicates:

- *Evaluation is, by definition, designed to improve faculty performance.*
- *It is conducted at intervals of no more than five years.*
- *A peer review committee undertakes the process.*

- *The peer group makes its evaluative criteria and procedure available to the faculty member beforehand.*
- *Student evaluations are included.*
- *A copy of the peer report is given to the evaluated professor.*
- *Written recommendations garnered by the peer review panel are provided to the evaluated professor.*
- *The chairman of the peer review panel meets to discuss the results of the report with the professor after evaluation.*
- *Grievance procedures are available to appeal the results of any evaluation* (Heller 1985b, p. 30).

Although post-tenure evaluation and collective bargaining do not inherently conflict (Heller 1985b; Kleingartner 1984), that assertion largely depends upon the union's endorsement of post-tenure evaluation. Once endorsed by the union, implementation can be easier than if mandated by an outside public without faculty or union involvement. What seems critical is a mutual understanding among administrators and faculty of the purpose and the benefits of post-tenure review.

Opposition to Post-tenure Evaluation

While advocates for post-tenure evaluation are convincing, those who question the need for it and object to any attempts to formalize it are equally persuasive. The University of Pittsburgh denounced the idea because it was seen as working against the inherent values that tenure establishes (Chait and Ford 1982). Some contend that such evaluation stifles academic freedom by pressuring "faculty members to conform, avoid controversial research subjects, or publish 'potboilers' to build up their publications records" (Perry 1983, p. 25).

Others seriously question whether the benefits justify the investment of time and money that such a process would require. Committee A of the AAUP voiced thoughtful concerns at its November 1983 meeting when it issued the following statement: "The Association believes that periodic formal institutional evaluation of each postprobationary faculty member would bring scant benefit, would widen unacceptable costs not only in money and time but also in a dampening of creativity and of collegial relationships, and would threaten academic freedom'' (AAUP 1983, p. 14a). Still others caution that it leads to erosion of collegial relationships, mistrust of one another, conformity instead of creativity, a devaluing of rigorous pretenure evaluations, and increased bureaucratization and centralized control (Bennett and Chater 1984; Larsen 1983; Moses 1985; Stern 1983).

In 1983, the American Council on Education (ACE) proposed a joint meeting—the Wingspread Conference—with the AAUP, offering invited faculty members, administrators, association officers from AAUP and ACE, and foundation executives a forum to discuss the National Commission on Higher Education Issues' 1982 proposal that institutions adopt formal periodic review procedures for tenured faculty.

A postconference statement suggested that a majority of participants were satisfied with the traditional procedures for assessing tenured faculty already in operation on most campuses, including formal and/or informal evaluation to determine promotion in rank, awards of sabbaticals, awards of research grants, faculty development grants, merit pay, outstanding teaching awards, and awards of endowed chairs (Kearl 1983). Advancing the argument that these informal methods of evaluation are valuable as well as endemic to academic life, one participant suggested that personnel strategies basic to the industrial model cannot be transferred to the academic model, claiming that ''periodic post-tenure review is inimical to collegiality and to the spirit of academic freedom'' (Stern 1983, p. 13a).

Likewise, the idea of a post-tenure evaluation system that carries the threat of sanctions was opposed on the basis that such sanctions are '' . . . unnecessary and inconsistent with [our] vital commitment to the conditions [that] nourish the spirit of free inquiry'' (Larsen 1983, p. 10a).

The consensus statements drafted by the participants represent one direction that future discussions on the issue might take:

1. *Along with the Commission, we reaffirm our commitment to academic tenure and the protections of academic freedom it provides. No system of faculty evaluation should be permitted to weaken or undermine those principles.*

2. *Institutional assessments of the teaching, research, and service programs of departments, schools, and other academic units should be made at regular intervals.*
3. *The performance of tenured faculty members is evaluated on a continuing basis, formal and informal, by their colleagues and students, by their peers in their disciplines at other institutions, and by potential funding agencies both public and private; we regard this continuing evaluation as healthy and indeed valuable.*
4. *The performance of tenured faculty members should be and normally is regularly evaluated by their institutions for some or all of the following purposes: distribution of merit salary increases, promotion, and institutional academic awards such as sabbaticals, research support, and teaching awards. Written descriptions of the purposes, criteria, and methods by which these evaluations are made should be provided to the faculty.*
5. *Decisions made as a result of these approaches to the evaluation and improvement of faculty performance should not be used as a ground to dismiss tenured faculty. Where grounds for dismissal are believed to exist, informal resolutions of the problem should be pursued first. If these fail, then existing due process procedures can be employed* (AAUP 1983, p. 14a).

Some conference participants also mentioned the concept of post-tenure evaluation as a catalyst for faculty development. Certain participants felt the benefits accrued could offset the risks involved, when they are viewed and designed as a means of nurturing faculty growth and excellence, encouraging faculty self-evaluation, and promoting institutional review of units and programs (Landini 1983; Larsen 1983; Shapiro 1983).

At issue here, though, seems to be an overarching distinction between what constitutes periodic evaluation (that is, scheduled and systematic) versus the other forms of faculty evaluation that occur at varying intervals on campus for purposes other than specific faculty and institutional renewal. The participants at the Wingspread Conference and others maintain that such types of customary, ongoing evaluation as outlined in the conference consensus statements are occurring and are quite sufficient. Those who argue in favor of a more systematic and comprehensive evaluation plan for tenured faculty appear to do so because they feel that the customary evaluations are not adequate in their emphasis on improvement or revitalization and that they tend to be of a "pro forma, often hit-or-miss, hurried character" (Bennett 1985, p. 65). Although it is true that many forms of assessment do occur normally in the form of merit awards, pay increases, and reviews of research requests, grants, and manuscripts, these assessments do not generally provide the feedback to the faculty member that is necessary for positive changes to occur (Bennett 1985, p. 67). The conclusion is that "at many institutions, too much energy is currently being spent on evaluation in ways that will not promote academic excellence, institutional integrity, or public confidence" (p. 68).

Summary

Academics are far from agreement about the merits of a formal process for post-tenure review. Approbation is counterbalanced by reservation and skepticism. While some observers voice serious questions about the necessity, the benefit, and the costs of such a periodic process, others suggest it can serve as a mechanism for the identification and remediation of deficiencies, a basis for merit pay decisions, and a catalyst for faculty renewal and development.

Clearly, it is in the context and spirit of faculty development that one finds the strongest and the most convincing justification for implementation of a periodic system for post-tenure evaluation. Yet, as those in the academy are keenly aware, advocacy in the philosophical sense does not automatically translate into operational efficacy.

What, if anything, is known about current institutional practices of post-tenure evaluation, their purposes, and their effectiveness? Does any evidence exist to dispel the disputations of those who believe that such processes are inimical to the traditions of tenure and academic freedom or to confirm the apparent convictions of those who see such processes as a means for faculty renewal and growth? Coe College and St. Lawrence University are two institutions that have initiated formal systems of post-tenure evaluation. Both developed their plans in response to concerns about tenure density.

At Coe College, the impetus for post-tenure review arose from heated faculty debate surrounding a board-supported tenure quota plan. In place of a quota, the faculty accepted a proposal for a non-tenure-track system to cover up to 10 percent of the full-time faculty as well as the establishment of a 10-year faculty growth and development plan. Faculty at Coe develop and submit a 10-year plan for professional growth and development at the time of tenure deliberations. If the faculty member is granted tenure, he or she updates and modifies that plan every five years thereafter. Further, the dean and department chair evaluate the faculty member's accomplishments in relationship to this plan at the same five-year intervals. This evaluation is complemented with input from students, peers, and outside experts. The 10-year plan and accompanying evaluation are used as input in making decisions related to promotion, merit pay, and professional leave. The revocation of tenure is not an option should performance be unsatisfactory, leading the dean at Coe College to view the process as "primarily a counseling tool" (Chait and Ford 1982, p. 178).

The revocation of tenure is not an option should performance be unsatisfactory, leading the dean . . . to view the process as "primarily a counseling tool."

At St. Lawrence University, an unsatisfactory post-tenure evaluation can lead to dismissal for cause. In lieu of adopting an alternative system to tenure, a faculty committee at St. Lawrence recommended that each faculty member be subject to review by the college's Committee on Professional Standards. The dean and department chair share the responsibility to ensure that each tenured faculty member's performance is reviewed every four years, unless the faculty member's performance has been reviewed for another purpose. The purpose of the review is to determine faculty effectiveness. If faculty incompetence is observed, actions can be taken that could result in termination, although to date no such actions have occurred. This post-tenure review occurs as "the most efficacious means to assure accountability" (Chait and Ford 1982, p. 180).

The reported usefulness of post-tenure evaluation at these two institutions lies as much in its process as in its product:

> *The evaluation process, subtly, almost subconsciously, creates an expectation of progress and advancement. Properly executed, the process enables individuals and departments to set directions and priorities in harmony with institutional objectives . . . . [Faculty interviewed] stressed the value of the plans as a means to orchestrate departmental activities and as a means to learn more about the interests and ambitions of colleagues* (Chait and Ford 1982, p. 183).

Three other institutional plans reported in the literature are those from Carlton College, Earlham College, and San Jose State University. Carlton College in Minnesota follows a rather novel approach to post-tenure evaluation. Through slight modifications in its existing evaluation process, the college envisions one-seventh of its tenured faculty reviewed each year, with the possibility of exemptions above a certain age. The procedures, however, would be the same as those outlined for the original decision on whether to confer tenure:

> *A list of 20–30 names of current and recently graduated students is solicited from the faculty member concerned, with appropriate balances among male/female, major/nonmajor, and performance levels of students in the faculty member's courses. A second list of names is obtained through a random sample, using similar distribution criteria. The Dean of the college writes to each student requesting the student's evaluation of the faculty member. The faculty member has seen the letter . . . the Dean is sending. Evaluations from current students are normally sought only when students are away from the campus. After the evaluations have been received, the Dean meets with the faculty member concerned to discuss the letters, reading all relevant information from the letters to the faculty member, though avoiding any*

references [that] might identify the author (Zuckert and Friedhoff 1980, p. 50).

The advantage of such a system is that it allows review of an individual faculty member rather than an individual course. It also frees the student evaluators from the pressures of peers and grades. More important, however, students do not respond to a prepared questionnaire but are asked to first write about the criteria they use in making judgments about an instructor's effectiveness and then to elaborate upon what the strengths and weaknesses of the faculty member in question are in light of the criteria used. Last, they are asked to offer strategies for the instructor's improvement. This assessment results in a private interview between the dean and the faculty member that is designed to "guarantee both a greater effectiveness to the evaluation and to respect the legitimate feelings of the individuals involved" (Zuckert and Friedhoff 1980, p. 50).

At Earlham College, evaluation of tenured faculty for the sole purpose of improvement is conducted every five years until the age of 60. The process is heavily steeped in review by colleagues. A committee of three colleagues, chosen by the dean and the faculty member, review the faculty member's portfolio, which contains a self-evaluation, evaluations by students, letters of support from colleagues, letters of support from present and past students, and other pertinent materials. In addition, the peer committee may request to observe the faculty member in the classroom. Together with the committee, the faculty member completes a self-assessment and develops a five-year plan. The committee sends a written report to the dean, who meets with the faculty member to discuss the five-year plan and the assessment. Institutional resources are made available to the faculty member as needed (Faculty Affairs Committee 1975). Earlham's plan is similar to those at Coe College and Carlton College insofar as revocation of tenure is not possible.

In the California State University system, "anyone who has not been reviewed for retention, tenure, or promotion for five years is subject to review of teaching and scholarship by a committee of his peers and an 'appropriate administrator' " (Galm 1985, p. 65). The specific procedures and criteria for post-tenure review are for the most part parallel to promotion review, but at San Jose State University, an alternative from the usual review process was successfully developed to include an initial series of five seminars with the tenured full professors subject for review. The seminars focused on course syllabi, objectives, grading criteria, audiovisual aids, classroom discussion techniques, and a specific discipline-based issue (Galm 1985). The result was the ability "to turn an onerous and perfunctory task into an experience [the participants] enjoyed and learned from" (p. 65). One tenured professor said:

> *"When I heard I was to be 'evaluated,' my first response was to assume that I would bear up, survive the ordeal with as much dignity as possible, and continue on afterwards, putting the whole thing out of my mind at the earliest opportunity. It was a real surprise to discover that the process actually had led me to rethink some of the classes I teach and to want to try some new things. That effect, I'm sorry to say, is something I never experienced when I was evaluated in years past for tenure and for my promotions"* (Galm 1985, p. 67).

To date, only two other studies have been undertaken specifically to investigate the status of formal post-tenure evaluation plans on college and university campuses (Bolden 1979; Licata 1984).

In the process of studying the 14 four-year public institutions in Alabama to determine whether systematic post-tenure evaluation existed, Bolden surveyed tenured and nontenured faculty and administrators from the same institutions to elicit their opinions and attitudes toward the concept of post-tenure review. In doing so, he separated administrators and faculty according to institutional level—that is, those in institutions granting doctorates from those in institutions granting master's degrees.

Approximately 68 percent of the overall administrative respondents indicated that they had policies to evaluate tenured faculty. After a review of the 14 campuswide faculty handbooks, however, Bolden found no formal institutionwide procedures outlined in the individual handbooks and concluded that the policies for post-tenure evaluation were established on a departmental rather than institutional basis. When asked to indicate what purpose or purposes

TABLE 1

PERCENTAGES OF ADMINISTRATORS* INDICATING A SPECIFIED PURPOSE OF WRITTEN POLICIES TO EVALUATE TENURED FACULTY

(N = 80)

Purpose	Category I (Doctoral Universities)	Category II (Master's Universities)	Combined
Merit increases	90.0	73.7	51.2
Evaluation of teaching performance	92.9	100.0	57.5
Contract renewal	47.6	50.0	23.7
Promotion in rank	96.8	89.5	60.0
Salary increase	89.7	77.8	50.0
Faculty development	85.2	47.4	41.2
Dismissal decisions	78.9	64.3	31.3

*Administrators comprised of academic deans (43.8 percent), department heads (52.5 percent), and others (3.7 percent).

Source: Bolden 1979, p. 30.

the post-tenure evaluation served, the respondents consistently indicated that it primarily served to evaluate teaching performance and as input for promotion in rank. The specific breakdown of all purposes mentioned in Bolden's study is shown in table 1.

Bolden concluded that "higher education faculty and administrators in Alabama support and believe that post-tenure evaluation policies should exist" (p. 90). He based this conclusion on the findings of his study, which indicated respondents believed:

- Periodic post-tenure reviews should be performed (84 percent).
- Administrators and tenured faculty colleagues together should evaluate tenured faculty (74.9 percent).
- Post-tenure evaluations will help a school or department be more responsible (81.1 percent).
- If a faculty member receives a poor post-tenure evaluation, the faculty member's position should be continued, but the faculty member should receive departmental support for improvement (87.4 percent).

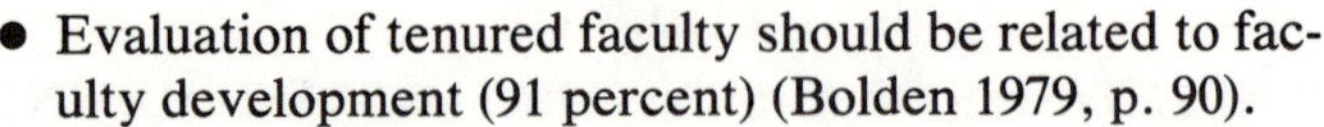

- Evaluation of tenured faculty should be related to faculty development (91 percent) (Bolden 1979, p. 90).

These findings were corroborated in a similar study of nine institutions belonging to the League for Innovation in the Community College (Licata 1984). Like the Alabama study, tenured and nontenured faculty and administrators were surveyed to determine the status of post-tenure evaluation at their selected institutions. The data from the study indicated that formal post-tenure evaluation existed in each of the nine participating community colleges. Perhaps more important, over 94 percent of respondents agreed that it should exist. The majority of administrators and faculty surveyed worked in institutions where the primary stated purpose for such evaluation was faculty development and improvement. And when asked what should be the primary purpose, the majority opinion remained unchanged. Table 2 displays administrators' and faculty members' responses to the stated and proposed institutional purposes for posttenure evaluation.

Licata concluded that in the community colleges surveyed, strong support existed for the concept of post-tenure evaluation as a mechanism for enhancing faculty development, basing this assumption in large part on the findings, which indicated respondents believed:

- Periodic post-tenure evaluation should be performed for tenured faculty to assess their level of performance and development needs (94 percent).
- Tenured faculty should welcome periodic assessment of their overall performance (94.5 percent).
- A faculty development program should be implemented in conjunction with the post-tenure evaluation plan (94.2 percent).
- Post-tenure evaluation increases the likelihood of faculty growth and vitality (81.4 percent).
- Multiple sources of input—from administrators, peers, students, and self—should be used for post-tenure evaluation (91.2 percent) (Licata 1984, pp. 135–37).

The data from this study also suggested, however, that the effectiveness of post-tenure evaluation in accomplishing its stated institutional purpose was somewhat uncertain

TABLE 2

STATED AND PROPOSED INSTITUTIONAL PURPOSES FOR POST-TENURE EVALUATION

	Administrators		*Faculty*	
	Present Stated Purpose	**Proposed Purpose**	**Present Stated Purpose**	**Proposed Purpose**
To provide information needed in making decisions for promotion, retention, dismissal, and normal salary increments	25.4	17.6	26.1	13.6
To provide information needed in making decisions about merit compensation	–	2.1	0.9	3.0
To provide a basis for individual faculty development and improvement	56.8	52.9	45.9	48.4
To provide each faculty member with diagnostic information concerning his or her instructional behavior and effectiveness	15.7	25.7	21.5	32.4
Other	2.2	1.6	5.7	2.6
No response	17.4	16.5	26.4	25.0

Source: Licata 1984.

for two reasons. First, the evaluation did not provide an effective mechanism to measure competence and incompetence; second, it paid only lip service to faculty development (pp. 130–32). This issue of effectiveness is critical and deserves attention in future studies.

Participants at the ACE Leadership Development Program on Periodic Review of Tenured Faculty were surveyed to determine the prevalence of post-tenure review at their institutions. (The results of that survey are presented in Appendix A.) More than half of the 31 responding institutions (public and private) reported an institutional system in place. In general, the process they followed included the development by the tenured faculty member of a portfolio or activity file that is then reviewed by a peer committee and the dean or by the dean alone. This review is used for decisions about salary, merit pay, or promotions in about 75 percent of the reported cases.

These two studies, albeit very limited in scope, when coupled with the earlier analysis by Chait and Ford (1982) lend some credence to the belief that post-tenure evaluation does exist to some degree and that a number of administrators and faculty in the field see benefit in the practice of formal periodic reviews of tenured faculty when directed specifically toward faculty development and promotion and not used as a mechanism for dismissal. The role that such evaluation can play in institutional self-regulation is also important to weigh. A movement toward national assessment in higher education seems imminent. Secretary of Education William J. Bennett recently noted that if "institutions don't assess their own performance, others—either state or commercial organizations—will" (*Higher Education and National Affairs* 1985). Add to this statement such recent initiatives as Accuracy in Academia and other attempts by outside publics to police academic ranks, and one is persuaded that individual institutions must find ways to initiate self-regulation before they are compelled to overcome attempts by others to do so.

Moving from what the literature conveys—that some four-year and two-year institutions are presently engaged in a formal process of post-tenure evaluation—leads to several questions: What components make up such evaluation plans? What criteria are used? What sources of input are included? What action occurs as a result of such evaluations?

Answers to such questions can be useful to institutions interested in entering into serious discussion about post-tenure review and for those wishing to explore possible ways to establish a system. A review of research and findings related to these questions from the larger field of faculty evaluation is necessary, because the process of post-tenure evaluation is a normal outgrowth of the process of pretenure evaluation.

Is it possible for a faculty evaluation plan to assess and assist at the same time, or must these processes be separate?

The Design of Post-tenure Evaluation

The history of formal faculty evaluation in higher education is still in its early stages. The tremendous student growth experienced on college campuses during the 1960s funneled energies in the direction of recruiting faculty and planning facilities. Administrative attention was devoted to managing expansion rather than methodically evaluating faculty. The financial plight of the 1970s, the public outcries for accountability, and the demands of faculty for a larger voice in decisions about tenure and promotion, however, have led institutions to look inward and to establish comprehensive evaluation procedures and personnel policies (Centra 1979; Miller 1972, 1974; Prodgers 1980; Seldin 1980, 1984; Whitman and Weiss 1982). The basic issue raised in discussions of evaluation is whether faculty evaluation serves a formative or summative purpose. In other words, is it possible for a faculty evaluation plan to assess and assist at the same time, or must these processes be separate?

Strong cases have been made that the overriding purpose for evaluation should be the improvement of instruction through faculty growth (Cohen 1974; Miller 1974) and that the only "useful thing [it] can do is to lend direction to the process of self-evaluation" (Cohen 1974, p. 20).

Some experts maintain that a distinct difference between the functions of evaluation and development is paramount (Aubrecht 1984; Seldin 1984), but separating evaluation (judgment) from development (assistance) proves more difficult than might be expected. When faculty and administrators in one study were asked whether a faculty evaluation scheme can both judge and assist, the responses were evenly divided: 50 percent responded "yes," and 50 percent responded "no" (Mark 1977). The researcher attributed the split to the difficulty in separating the two goals on an operational level.

Such separation of goals may not really be necessary, however (O'Connell and Smartt 1979). What is requisite is a conceptual framework on which to base an evaluation system. Once such a framework is established, questions of judgment and assistance can be better answered.

The literature on faculty evaluation, however, plentiful as it is, has paid parsimonious attention to the design and implementation of a system specifically geared for the evaluation of tenured faculty. It thus becomes necessary to extrapolate from the plethora of pretenure evaluation models. In and of itself, this requirement should not necessarily be cast in a negative light, because the basic areas of faculty responsibility (teaching, research, and public service) have remained fairly constant over the years. What changes with time are institutional emphases and individual interest and demonstrated ability in the three areas. In this way, then, evaluation is viewed as a continuum from pre- to post-tenure status, with the assumption that "the fundamental approach to faculty evaluation should not change materially as a function of tenure status; the evaluation of tenured faculty should represent a continuation of prior practices" (Chait and Ford 1982, p. 174). What then are these prior faculty evaluation practices, and should they be altered when fashioned to the needs of post-tenure evaluation?

Evaluation Models and Practices

Important conceptual models for faculty evaluation are found in the works of several evaluation theorists (Case 1971; Centra 1979; Dressel 1976; Edwards 1974; Miller 1972, 1974; Seldin 1980, 1984; Southern Regional Education Board 1977). These models are more similar than dissimilar, offering five principles of evaluation applicable to faculty assessment both before and after tenure is awarded and recommended as a basis for a post-tenure evaluation plan:

1. The need for a clearly defined purpose
2. The need for multiple sources of input to the evaluation
3. The need to identify areas and criteria to be assessed
4. The need to agree on measurable standards
5. The need for a flexible and individualized evaluation plan.

The need for a clearly defined purpose

The purpose of evaluation is to provide information that will assist with a faculty member's development and help to improve instruction and that will assist in personnel decisions related to tenure, promotion, retention, and salary. Writers do not agree, however, whether one purpose supersedes or excludes the other, some believing that the developmental animus should be the only basis for evaluation (Case 1971; Dressel 1976; Miller 1972; Moses 1985) and others suggesting that the litigious nature of personnel decisions and constraints on time and resources force institutions to use evaluation in both a formative (improvement) and summative (evaluative) way (Centra 1979; Seldin 1980, 1984; SREB 1977). Hence, although faculty evaluation serves dual purposes, in the long run it aims at improving instruction.

As institutions consider the possibility of formal post-tenure evaluation, the need for a clearly defined and articulated purpose cannot be overemphasized. The purpose must be specific, free of a hidden agenda, educational, and related directly to the process (Moses 1985). Further, clear definition of purpose is important because the purpose determines who evaluates faculty. Presently, a formative evaluation system seems to hold the most value and promise to institutions concerned with vitality and renewal.

The need for multiple sources of input

Evaluation theorists unanimously agree that an evaluation system needs multiple sources of input. Disagreement arises, however, over the weight each source should carry in the final decision (Dressel 1976; Miller 1972, 1974; Smith 1976; SREB 1977). This discordance originates from the contradictory nature of the various sources called upon to judge faculty competence.

Research has uncovered advantages and disadvantages of every evaluation component used but has failed to identify a consistent and generalizable system that can be applied to all colleges, to all decisions, and to each evidence. . . . Each component has its strengths, its weaknesses, its objectivity, and its biases (Mark 1977, p. 2).

The sources of input generally used in faculty evaluation plans are administrative evaluation, peer evaluation, student evaluation, and self-evaluation.

Administrative evaluation. Administrative ratings correlate more to peer ratings than to student ratings (Kulik 1974); high correlation has been reported between administrative and peer ratings, low correlation between administrative and student ratings (Greenwood and Ramagli 1980). Traditionally, administrative appraisal, primarily conducted by the dean and the department chair, involved classroom observation, examination of course materials, or review of students' and/or peers' ratings. Unfortunately, this approach often used "informal and unsystematic sources of information" (Greenwood and Ramagli 1980, p. 679). Today, administrative evaluation is still a major influence in evaluation plans, but its importance has been somewhat diminished by the inclusion of other participants (Mark 1977; Seldin 1984), and administrators, particularly department chairs, are seen today as the coordination point or integrating force for the faculty evaluation system (Bevan 1982; Eble 1982).

Evaluation by colleagues and peers. Although a sensitive area, evaluation by colleagues and peers finds support on many campuses and in the literature (Centra 1979; Dressel 1976; Seldin 1980; Whitman and Weiss 1982). Basically, colleagues play two roles—individual and collective—in the process. Peers provide evidence individually to assess the quality of teaching, research, and scholarship by classroom visitation, examination of instructional materials, or completion of a rating instrument. Collectively, they provide aggregate judgments of performance through peer departmental committees (Centra 1979; Cohen and McKeachie 1980; Seldin 1980). For some, the benefit derived from including colleagues' evaluations in the total design lies in a peer's certain ability to appraise some aspects of effective teaching, scholarship, and research (Batista 1976; French-Lazovik 1981; Whitman and Weiss 1982); it has been suggested that peers provide the most effective evaluation of course content (Miller 1972).

The validity and reliability of peer ratings are difficult to measure, however, because so little research has been conducted in this area (Dressel 1976; Whitman and Weiss 1982). One study suggests that when peer ratings are compared to student ratings, their reliability is low. Not only are colleagues more generous in ratings than students, but the correlation among the various colleague ratings is low (Centra 1975). This low correlation can be altered, however, if visitations to a classroom are made more frequently (Centra 1979; Seldin 1980). Other research has reported fairly high correlations between student ratings and peer ratings (Greenwood and Ramagli 1980; Kulik 1974). The validity of colleagues' evaluation of teaching suffers from the same bias that students' evaluations do: Good ratings do not necessarily equate with good teaching. Popularity and politics can influence a rating (Whitman and Weiss 1982).

Although "the evidence . . . based primarily on classroom observation would in most instances not be reliable enough to use in making decisions in tenure and promotion" (Centra 1975, p. 327), some essential guidelines for a peer review system incorporate classroom observation:

1. *Colleague observation is a component, and only a component, in the system of teacher evaluation. Its aim must be clearly defined and understood by students, faculty, and administrators.*
2. *Faculty resistance is a fact of campus life and can best be met by disarming and/or sympathetic understanding at open forums.*
3. *There is no substitute for goodwill, mutual trust, respect, and support, and both the institution and faculty must strive for these ends if classroom observation is to be successful.*
4. *The primary purpose of colleague evaluation is the improvement of teaching and learning.*
5. *If the information is carefully gathered, promptly reported, and judiciously interpreted, colleague eval-*

uation based in part on classroom observation is capable of solid judgments on merit increases, promotion, and tenure.

6. *Avoid burdening classroom visitation with bureaucratic complexity. Keep the system simple, clear, acceptable to the observing colleague and the teacher he is observing. Train the colleague in what and how to observe. Explain the results to the teacher and use them judiciously* (Seldin 1980, pp. 74–75).

Most authorities agree that evaluations by colleagues should be but one component in the overall process of evaluation (Centra 1979; Dressel 1976; Seldin 1980, 1984; Smith 1976); a formative post-tenure evaluation scheme, by its very nature, depends on input from colleagues.

Evaluations by students. Probably no evaluation issue has received more attention over the years than the issue of student ratings. Are they reliable, valid, stable, and useful in evaluating faculty competence? While conflicting pieces of research exist, most evaluation specialists now recognize the ability of students to judge fairly. Consequently, inclusion of student ratings is one of the most widely used components in evaluation systems (Benton 1982; Centra 1979; Cohen and McKeachie 1980; Kronk and Shipka 1980; Miller 1974; Seldin 1980).

The data generated from these ratings are used in several ways: (1) to assist institutions in rendering judgments regarding tenure or promotion and continued employment; (2) to help to stimulate the improvement of instruction by providing information that instructors can use to improve teaching and learning; (3) to help students choose courses and instructors (Benton 1982; Centra 1979; Gillmore 1983–84; Miller 1974).

Despite the fact that nearly half of all institutions of higher education use student ratings, faculty and administrators still continue to express much skepticism regarding their suitability. The basis for this skepticism is the belief that it is impossible to define effective teaching and difficult to identify a criterion against which student ratings can be compared. Some also object to the impersonal procedures used in gathering students' rating data (Menges 1979) and to the fact that many of the rating instruments used have been developed by people not qualified to construct such instruments (Costin, Greenough, and Menges 1971).

Literally hundreds of student assessment instruments are reported in the literature. With so many forms in existence, standardization of criteria is far from possible, but some similarities are beginning to emerge. The importance of understanding the issues related to evaluation by students should not be underplayed in a discussion of periodic review of tenured faculty, especially if such evaluations are used directly in making employment decisions. "If student ratings are to qualify as evidence in support of faculty employment decisions, questions concerning their reliability and validity must be addressed" (Gillmore 1983–84, p. 561).

- *What should students be asked?*

Some writers assert that students should comment only on those aspects of teaching that they can legitimately assess (Marquis, Lane, and Dorfman 1979; Menges 1979): (1) classroom events (pace of presentation, the instructor's availability to students outside of class, the use of examples, the requirement to apply knowledge learned); (2) individual progress (the individual's perceptions of progress in meeting course objectives); and (3) the student's satisfaction (willingness to take another course from the instructor, willingness to recommend the instructor to a friend, value of the course) (Menges 1979, p. 361). In one review of evaluation studies, students identified those characteristics that they felt were indicators of good teaching (Feldman 1976). The items reported most consistently were the instructor's ability to stimulate interest and the instructor's clarity of presentation. Other characteristics reported often were the instructor's knowledge of the subject matter, preparation for class, enthusiasm for teaching, and interaction with students (pp. 263–64).

- *What form should the questions take?*

Although the most popular format for obtaining feedback from students is the prepared questionnaire, it may not necessarily be the most efficient or helpful strategy, particularly if a candid and thoughtful diagnosis of a teacher's strengths and weaknesses is sought. Other modes might be more useful:

1. Group interview of students by an instructor or a third party to discuss students' opinions about the instructor and the course
2. Students' narration of thoughts while completing a prepared questionnaire
3. Students' written comments to an open-ended list of questions
4. Training students to observe and record classroom events as a basis for discussion with the instructor
5. A meeting of an advisory group with the instructor after soliciting students' reactions to courses (Menges 1979, pp. 362–63).

- *How valid are ratings by students?*

The literature is replete with research studies that attempt to examine the validity of student ratings by using a construct validation approach in which student ratings are related to another measure that is assumed to indicate effective teaching. This measure might be student achievement, faculty self-evaluation, peer ratings, administrative ratings, or retrospective ratings by alumni (Marsh and Overall 1980).

A recent meta-analysis of student ratings and student achievement, for example, concluded that an average correlation exists between high student ratings and high student achievement; that is, the instructors who received the highest ratings were those whose students achieved the most (Cohen 1981, p. 296). Another study (Marsh and Overall 1980), which used a cognitive criterion (standard exam performance) and an affective criterion (self-reported measure of students' ability to apply course materials) to measure the validity of ratings, however, showed that students' learning, as assessed by a final examination, was not highly correlated with the instructor's overall rating or the overall course rating but that the affective criterion was highly correlated with the overall course rating.

A review of published validity studies paints an even more pessimistic picture (Dowell and Neal 1982). The analysis shows that the literature yields "unimpressive" estimates of the validity of student ratings, suggesting that the validity is modest at best and quite variable, depending on students' characteristics.

While researchers do not agree about the validity of ratings by students, they do agree that "confusion in the literature does not justify abolition of ratings" (Dowell and Neal 1982, p. 61) and that ratings are useful but should not be the only criterion used (Cohen 1983).

A modest relationship seems to exist between students' evaluations of individual faculty and those same faculty members' self-evaluations (Centra 1972; Seldin 1982). A recent study, for example, showed good agreement between students and instructors as to what constitutes effective teaching: (1) learning/value, (2) enthusiasm, (3) organization, (4) group interaction, (5) individual rapport, (6) breadth of coverage, (7) exams/grading, (8) assignments, (9) workload/difficulty (Marsh 1982). Centra (1972) recommended that "as an aid to instructional improvement, teacher self ratings . . . be used in conjunction with student feedback as a means of highlighting discrepancies for the individual instructor" (p. 50).

On the other hand, the accord between peer ratings and student ratings is uneven, and

> *. . . colleague ratings of teaching effectiveness based primarily on classroom observation would in most instances not be reliable enough to use in making decisions on tenure and promotion* (Centra 1975, p. 327).

- *How reliable are ratings by students?*

Less attention has been given to studies of reliability than to validity, but generally the reliability of student ratings is positive, especially when class sizes are reasonable (Greenwood and Ramagli 1980, p. 673). A study of the correlation between students' end-of-term ratings and follow-up ratings (one year after graduation) found a high correlation between them and concluded that stability is not altered by emotional distance or a different situation (Marsh and Overall 1980). In any event, when ratings by students are used in employment decisions, ratings from a sample of courses taught by the instructor, preferably from

When ratings by students are used in employment decisions, ratings from a sample of courses taught by the instructor . . . should be used to increase reliability.

five to ten classes, should be used to increase reliability (Gillmore 1983–84, p. 563).

- *How useful are student ratings?*

Some agreement is evident among faculty that student ratings can be useful as a source of feedback, but far less agreement is evident about whether this feedback does indeed lead to improved instruction. The usefulness and value of such ratings in personnel decision making is not clear.

The "use to be made of the results dictates their form" (Menges 1979, p. 363). In other words, if their main intent is for decisions about tenure, promotion, or salary, the information must be painstakingly accurate to avert a lawsuit and should include norms for comparisons. On the other hand, if the ratings are to improve instruction, the data should be channeled directly to the faculty member and might include data collection over the course of the term rather than all at once.

The results of an investigation of faculty members' perceptions of the usefulness of objective questionnaires, open-ended questions, and group interviews indicated that faculty unanimously regarded the information gathered by the three methods to be most useful, accurate, and credible when used for self-improvement (Ory and Braskamp 1981). Faculty also generally wanted more than one type of feedback and rated the information garnered from a group interview as the most comprehensive and written comments the least comprehensive (p. 277).

- *Can feedback from students positively change instructional practices if approached properly?*

Centra (1972), in his pioneer research of this same question, found that changes could be effected only for teachers who had unrealistically high opinions of their teaching effectiveness as compared to the students' opinions. Teachers who viewed themselves as average or poor did not change. It should be noted, though, that the teachers in Centra's study were not provided with any outside interpretation of results or supervisory assistance related to strategies to make corresponding changes or improvements.

Another study to determine the value of students' feedback to college instructors showed that the feedback did not seem to have any significant effects on the instructor's performance (Rotem 1978) but that:

> *To be effective, feedback must contain diagnostic information that helps the teacher know not only whether or not his performance is considered satisfactory, but also the particular areas in which he has to improve* (p. 317).

The heartening message to supervisors was that "educational consulting services might have to become an integral part of evaluation aimed at improved teaching" (p. 317).

A meta-analysis of the findings from 22 separate research studies dealing with the effect of student ratings on improving instruction found that feedback from student ratings can make a "modest but significant contribution to the improvement of college teaching" (Cohen 1980, p. 336), if feedback is augmented. In any event, the research related to student ratings suggests that they are useful but should not be the only component used in evaluating faculty. Alternative strategies to a prepared rating form may have some appeal and merit when used in post-tenure evaluation. Consultation in connection with the student feedback is important in post-tenure evaluation because improved instruction is presumably an important aspect and outgrowth of faculty evaluation.

Self-evaluation. Self-evaluation encourages a faculty member to examine his or her own performance and to note strengths and weaknesses. Although this technique is not presently practiced extensively in higher education (Mark 1977), increasing support for its use and recognition of its value can be found in the literature (Burson 1982; Cohen 1974; Dressel 1976; Miller 1974; Seldin 1980; Whitman and Weiss 1982).

Faculty tend to rate themselves higher than students, peers, and administrators rate them (Blackburn and Clark 1975; Greenwood and Ramagli 1980), leading those in the field to recommend that self-evaluation be combined with other types of ratings to enhance its usefulness.

Another concern leveled against self-evaluation is that it suffers from its singular nature. Peer and student evaluations tend to be composite ratings; therefore, inordinately high and low ratings tend to offset one another (Smith 1976). Studies indicate that self-evaluation is not particularly useful in decisions about tenure, promotion, or salary but can be very helpful in development (Centra 1979). Institutions interested in a developmental mode for post-tenure evaluation should consider the value and perhaps the necessity of including self-evaluation.

In sum, the use of multiple data sources to provide accumulated evidence of performance seems wise, because the present research base does not indicate that any measure used alone is sufficiently valid, particularly for summative post-tenure evaluations. Further, in the development of a post-tenure evaluation plan, institutions must decide who conducts the evaluation. Review by a panel or committee of peers should play prominently in the evaluation, although the department chair and/or dean continue to be crucial to the success of the total evaluation process (Bennett and Chater 1984; Moses 1985).

The need to identify areas and criteria to be assessed

While observers generally agree that the three broad areas of teaching, research, and service make up the traditional three-legged academic stool upon which evaluation is based, the amount of emphasis each area receives is not constant and depends on institutional mission and priority (Eble 1982). The question of emphasis is especially salient to the design of post-tenure evaluations; evaluation systems should measure and emphasize those areas that in reality an institution values and rewards.

Table 3 (p. 52–53) displays the criteria institutions used in pretenure evaluation as reported in the literature from 1966 to 1984. Where possible, the rank order of the criteria from these research studies are presented to indicate importance or frequency of inclusion in evaluation plans. Table 3 also includes available research on criteria used in post-tenure evaluations. The rank order of these results is also listed.

Bolden's results, when compared to the results of the research studies of Astin and Lee (1967), Centra (1976, 1979), Gustad (1961), Seldin (1980, 1984), and the Southern Regional Education Board (1977), demonstrate no great differences among the major reported criteria used in pretenure evaluation and those recommended for post-tenure

tenure evaluation and those recommended for post-tenure evaluation. In all studies, classroom teaching/teaching effectiveness consistently ranks as the area most frequently included in evaluations. Seven of the ten criteria chosen most frequently for inclusion in post-tenure evaluations from Bolden's study were also most frequently mentioned in six of the pretenure evaluation studies found in table 3: classroom teaching, research, service on a departmental committee, service on an institutional committee, academic advising, general service, and publications. Availability to students, cooperation, and students' rating appeared only in Bolden's study.

Licata's study (1984) focused on those criteria presently used in community college post-tenure evaluation plans. The results are in concert with the earlier pretenure studies noted in table 3 and with studies by Mark (1977) and the Southern Regional Education Board (1977) that showed that the major criteria favored in New York and in southern community colleges revolve around instruction, instruction-related activities, and student advisement. Those criteria noted most frequently in Licata's study include classroom teaching, attendance and reliability, innovation in teaching methods and materials, service on departmental committees, and course or curriculum development. It is clear from table 3 that Licata's study supports the importance of classroom instruction and instruction-related activities (innovation in teaching methods, course and curriculum development work) but does not evidence strong support for student advising. Likewise, because of the historical institutional mission of the community college as primarily a teaching institution, one would expect that research, publication, consultation, and other activities associated with four-year and graduate degree–granting institutions would not receive prominent attention in a community college evaluation scheme. What is notable in the Licata study, however, is that administrators chose the same five criteria as faculty as the most influential in the post-tenure evaluation plan. Furthermore, when faculty and administrators were asked what criteria they preferred to be the most influential, the responses were unchanged and identical to those indicated as presently the most influential. Moreover, faculty and administrators generally disagree with the statement that "the criteria used to evaluate

What is notable . . . is that administrators chose the same five criteria as faculty as the most influential in the post-tenure evaluation plan.

TABLE 3

FACULTY EVALUATION CRITERIA IN PRETENURE AND POST-TENURE EVALUATION STUDIES*

	Pretenure Evaluation Studies									Post-tenure Evaluation Studies		
Criteria	AAUP/AAC 1973	Astin & Lee 1967*	Centra 1976* 1979	Dressel 1976	Gustad 1961*	Miller 1974	Seldin 1980*	Seldin 1984*	SREB 1977*	Bolden 1979*	Licata 1984* A_1	Licata 1984* F_2
Classroom teaching/ effectiveness	x	1	1	x	1	x	1	1	1	1	1	1
Availability to students						x				2	9	6
Research	x	4	4	x	5	x	6	5	5	3	18	18
Service on departmental committee	x	8	6	x	7	x	3		3	4	4	4
Service on institutional committee	x	8	6	x	7	x	3	3	3	5	11	10
Academic advising		7	7		4	x	2	2	2	6	10	11
Cooperation	x					x				7		
Student rating	x			x						8		
General service		10	11	x	10	x	8			9		
Publication	x	6	3,5	x	6	x	8	6	6	10	17	15
Membership in professional organizations		19	9	x	8	x	7	7	6	11	13	13
Support of departmental policy										12		
Supervision of graduate study		5	8	x	11	x	10	10		13		
Service to community	x	10	11	x	10	x	9	9	8	14	12	12
Personal attributes	x	2	10		3	x	5	8	4	15	7	7
Elected office in organizations						x				16		

TABLE 3 continued

Length of service in rank	3		9	x	4	4	17		
Consultation	13	12	12		12	11		14	14
Competing job offers	11	13	13		13	13		19	19
Professional qualifications		2							
Supervision of honors	12		14		11	11			
Other			2						
Attendance and reliability								2	2
Innovation in teaching methods/materials								3	3
Course or curriculum development								5	5
Accumulation of graduate credits								6	8
Working toward doctorate								8	9
Teaching community service or office campus courses								15	16
Personal lifestyle								16	17

* Rank order of criteria noted if available from study.
x Included in faculty evaluation system, no rank order available.
A_1 Administrative response.
F_2 Faculty response.

Astin and Lee (1967): 484 institutions, including colleges and universities of varying sizes.
Centra (1976, 1979): 134 institutions, including research universities, doctoral-granting universities, and comprehensive universities.
Gustad (1961): 584 institutions, including four-year liberal arts colleges, private universities, public universities, state colleges, and junior colleges.
Seldin (1980): 680 institutions, all four-year liberal arts colleges. Deans responded to survey.
Seldin (1984): 616 institutions, all four-year liberal arts colleges. Deans responded to survey.
SREB (1977): 536 institutions in 14 southern states. All four- and two-year institutions included. Presidents responded to survey.

tenured faculty should differ from criteria used to evaluate nontenured faculty.''

Some interesting patterns have emerged over the past 10 years in the factors used to evaluate faculty in liberal arts colleges (Seldin 1984). While teaching performance has remained constant as the most important consideration in evaluation, publication, research, public service, and activity in professional societies have become increasingly important. These activities bring visibility to the campus and help to garner funding from outside sources. Conversely, factors such as personal attributes, length of service in rank, and competing job offers tend to receive less emphasis today, probably because they tend to be less job specific. Curiously, student advisement seems to be waning in importance in public institutions, where numbers of students continue to grow, but is still considered important on private campuses, where attracting and keeping students is integral to continued existence (Seldin 1984).

In general, the spectrum of faculty activities that are included in faculty evaluations has expanded over the years. One explanation for this apparent expanse is an attempt by institutions to become more systematic and more interested in the reliability and scope of information collected (Seldin 1984).

From the limited research base available, the criteria used in pretenure faculty evaluation seem to carry over to post-tenure evaluation. Nevertheless, each institution needs to determine the amount of emphasis each is given.

The need to agree on measurable standards

Consensus about what areas or criteria should be included in an evaluation plan is only one part of the evaluation triad. What constitutes quality in each of the areas and who is qualified to judge such quality must also be agreed upon (Centra 1979; Miller 1972, 1974; Seldin 1980, 1984; SREB 1977).

After studying faculty evaluation processes in 536 post-secondary institutions in 14 southern states, the Southern Regional Education Board concluded that ''standards may be the most difficult element to develop and put into effect at the institutional level since many institutions seem accustomed to stating standards broadly'' (1977, p. 421). The SREB recommended that if standards for each area, function, or criterion cannot be agreed upon, then the appropriateness of including the area, function, or criterion in the education plan should be seriously questioned (SREB 1977).

The tendency today is to categorize the standards assigned to performance into two broad headings: criterion-referenced standards and norm-referenced standards. Criterion-referenced standards imply that the faculty member's performance is gauged against preestablished measures, resulting in the assignment of a qualitative or quantitative descriptor. While most institutions tend to use criterion-based measures, care is needed in explaining what the chosen descriptors mean (Miller 1972; SREB 1977).

Norm-referenced standards, on the other hand, mean that a faculty member's performance is compared to that of a norm group, generally one's peers. Institutions generally use this approach when constraints dictate that only a preestablished percentage of a cohort can receive a promotion, merit increase, or tenure status.

Both of these measures are aimed at formulating qualitative judgments regarding faculty performance. But what constitutes such quality in teaching, research/scholarship, and service? If post-tenure evaluation is to serve a developmental aim, then the question of what constitutes quality must be answered.

Quality of teaching. More is written today about the sources of information used in assessing overall teaching performance than about the standards used by those sources of input to assess teaching performance (Astin and Lee 1967; Centra 1979; Mark 1977; Miller 1972, 1974; Seldin 1980, 1984; SREB 1977).

Regardless of the sources of information used, the underlying question of how one defines effective teaching remains at the heart of the issue. Over the years, this topic has provoked infinite hours of academic sparring, and the sparring is certain to continue. Some suggest that student achievement is the only criterion that should measure teaching effectiveness (Cohen and Brawer 1969; Rose 1976; Seldin 1980), but others suggest that teaching can be divided into a series of discrete activities to be measured and evaluated best by different constituency groups (Centra 1979; Miller 1972; Seldin 1980).

A three-dimensional approach to measuring teaching effectiveness has been suggested that involves evaluation of content expertise, institutional delivery skills, and instructional design skills (Aleomoni 1984). Content expertise translates into currency-in-discipline and a knowledge of subject matter, probably best judged by peers or the department chair. Instructional delivery skills refers to those characteristics of an instructor that promote learning and classroom interaction. Present students and former students can best appraise this dimension, and classroom visits by peers or department chair also address the question. Last, instructional design skills include the processes of developing course objectives, development of methods and materials to facilitate instruction, and development of the evaluation strategies necessary to measure changes in learning. Examinations by peers, the department chair, or the administration of syllabi and examinations lend themselves to judging this aspect (Aleomoni 1984).

The descriptors used in any form of teaching evaluation generally tend to be either very precise, as manifested by numerical ratings or measured changes in students' learning, or nonquantifiable, as indicated by subjective descriptions. Some research studies suggest that little agreement exists among college professors on how to objectively measure teaching effectiveness and that the standards used are either undefined or are defined in very subjective terms (Moomaw 1977b; Schulman and Trudell 1972). Thus, attempts have been made to deal with the issue of subjectivity by identifying nonsubjective criteria. Suggestions from one study advise institutions to use the following teaching criteria—ability to relate to students, ability to arouse interest, friendliness, empathy, and knowledge of subject matter (Schulman and Trudell 1972)—and another recommended the following eight broad groups to be used in evaluating teachers—"skill of instructor, student-teacher interaction, course organization and content, feedback to students, course difficulty/workload, motivation, importance of course, and attitude of instructor" (Benton 1982, p. 34).

It is incumbent upon institutions to decide what factors related to teaching should be evaluated and against what standards (Centra 1979; Miller 1972, 1974; SREB 1977; Whitman and Weiss 1982). One post-tenure evaluation study concluded that criteria used in post-tenure evaluation need to be more specific and objective, helping to reduce the subjectivity of the process (Licata 1984).

Quality of research and scholarship. The same issue of quality and how to measure it applies to faculty scholarship and research. It is understood that institutional affiliation and mission greatly affect the emphasis given to research in the evaluation process. We know, for example, that private liberal arts colleges stress research less than public liberal arts colleges (Seldin 1980, 1984) and that community colleges rarely stress it at all (Cohen and Brawer 1982; Licata 1984).

In the early days of faculty evaluation in most types of institutions, the faculty member's resume was the major mechanism used to measure quality of research (Gustad 1961). Later, the measures used in research universities, doctoral-granting universities, and comprehensive universities and colleges included the number of articles published in quality journals, the number of sole- or senior-authored books, and the quality of scholarly research and publications as judged by peers at the institution (Centra 1979). In liberal arts colleges recently, the trend is to consider with more frequency many types of information related to research and scholarship (Seldin 1984). While major emphasis continues to be on the number of sole- or senior-authored or edited books and articles in quality journals, monographs, chapters in books, publication in all professional journals, and papers presented at professional meetings are emphasized increasingly. In addition, while peers and the department chair are most frequently the judges of quality, honors or awards from the profession are also gaining in acceptance.

Quality of service. Very little is written about the assessment of service. Many institutions rely only on a listing of committee work, with scant measurement of the quality and dedication of the faculty member to the committee or other institutional assignments. Some guidelines may be useful to institutions hoping to better assess this area, including peers' assessment of how the faculty member accepts various service assignments, the quality of his contributions and work with committees, the effectiveness of a committee chair in conducting the meetings and keeping on target, the quality of the faculty member's relations with departmental colleagues, and evidence of a cooperative attitude toward department and institution (Seldin 1980).

Arriving at institutional consensus is essential in the consideration of which criteria should be included in a post-tenure evaluation, how each is measured, and by what standards, and that consensus can best be accomplished by faculty and administrative teamwork. Institutions wishing to modify their measures of quality as applied to teaching, research and scholarship, and service may find the rating forms and checklists developed by other institutions and researchers helpful (see, for example, Braskamp et al. 1983; Centra 1979; Miller 1972, 1974; Seldin 1980; SREB 1977; Whitman and Weiss 1982). Appendix B contains a sampling of sources for such rating instruments.

What must be kept in the forefront is the apparent tendency of the courts not to focus on the appropriateness of evaluation criteria but rather on the fairness of application. Thus, "the need for fair and reasonable procedures remains the responsibility of academic units" (Gillmore 1983–84, p. 576). Yet nowhere does the literature critically pursue these questions: What should be the expected standards of performance for tenured faculty? Are they the same as for receipt of tenure? Are they more or less? Some observers have expressed the perception that performance standards used in deliberations about promotion and tenure are in the process of escalation. In the Project on Reallocation previously mentioned, for example, approximately 68 percent of the respondents perceived that between 1977 and 1982, tenure was more difficult to acquire, and 61 percent assigned this trend to more stringent application of existing criteria or the formulation of new, stricter criteria (Bagshaw 1985, p. 17). About two-thirds of the faculty surveyed in another study reported that they perceived tenure to be harder to gain now than it was five years ago (Carnegie Foundation 1985).

"The concept of rising standards is difficult to define with precision because of the vagueness of academic hiring and promotion criteria" (Lee 1985, p. 357). Regardless of what interpretation is given to rising standards, however, "it is clear that many colleges and universities are requiring faculty seeking tenure or promotion, or candidates for faculty positions, to perform, in both qualitative and quantitative terms, at a level [that] had not been required of individuals promoted or tenured a decade earlier'' (p. 358).

If this statement is true, does a performance gap exist between recently tenured faculty and those tenured a decade ago? Because both pretenure and post-tenure performance criteria must be developed within the context of the individual institution, the question of what the expected performance standards for tenured faculty should be must also be negotiated in light of the campus climate and institutional mission. If a gap exists because of rising standards, a formative post-tenure evaluation process may help narrow the chasm by providing reinforcement and remediation to those faculty whose performance is deemed substandard.

The need for a flexible and individualized evaluation plan

Of equal importance to establishment of criteria, however, is the need for some degree of individualization in the choice of those criteria. Institutions that are mindful of individual faculty interests and needs as well as institutional priorities benefit from a post-tenure evaluation plan that can mesh commonly held evaluative criteria with individual faculty interests and abilities. How might this synchronization be accomplished? Three strategies appear necessary if equilibrium is to be achieved: (1) an institutional awareness and understanding of adult development theory and faculty career development theory; (2) an institutional commitment to link evaluation with faculty development; and (3) an institutional willingness to explore novel approaches, such as growth contracts, to accomplish this link between evaluation and development.

Theories of adult and career development. Theories of adult development have received mounting attention over the past decade because of their potential usefulness in human resource planning and development (Erikson 1978; Gould 1978; Levinson 1978; Sheehy 1976). The underlying message in each adult development model is that human beings continue to grow and develop during the adult years and that that growth is characterized by movement in and out of stages that are fraught with challenges and crises, transition and stability (Brookes and German 1983, p. 14).

The implications of these adult development theories have been considered and applied to various adult career stages. As a result, an expanding body of knowledge commonly referred to as career development theory tells us that one's career life is not static but takes on an evolving nature (Baldwin and Blackburn 1981). So too are academic careers characterized by various transitional stages: periods of high motivation, growth, doubt, decreasing competitiveness, and changing professional priorities and interests (see, for example, Baldwin 1979; Baldwin and Blackburn 1981; Braskamp, Fowler, and Ory 1984; Furniss 1981; Hodgkinson 1974). And "the policies and practices of colleges and universities must be flexible enough to accommodate the different vocational situations of professors at successive career stages" (Baldwin 1979, p. 18). A further complication is that although faculty desire autonomy and opportunities for diversity and complexity, they suffer under pressures of time and an inability to take risks (McKeachie 1983, pp. 64–65).

How to capitalize on this burgeoning research base of faculty/career development theory is of keen interest to practitioners in the field, particularly those entrusted with institutional planning and evaluation. Recognition that diversity exists among faculty is but the first step. Attempts to relate such diversity to a career development model that benefits the individual and institution must be based on an organizational willingness to:

- *. . . pay greater attention to the characteristics and concerns of each phase of the academic career*
- *. . . maintain the flexibility necessary to encourage professional growth*
- *. . . treat every individual as a unique individual* (Baldwin and Blackburn 1981, p. 608).

Based on this approach, it may not be advisable or efficacious for institutions to standardize evaluation criteria.

Faculty development as an outgrowth of evaluation. If, in fact, an institution's post-tenure evaluation plan should be changed to better accommodate faculty members' interests and department/division goals, one way to stimulate institutional resiliency and faculty vitality is through effective faculty development programs that promote an organizational environment in which faculty have ample opportunities to grow, retool, change careers, and increase job satisfaction. Formative post-tenure evaluation can serve as the link to such faculty development efforts.

Post-tenure review should have a direct link to faculty development and should not operate in isolation from faculty development practices (Bolden 1979). Certain obstacles can obstruct the tie between faculty evaluation and faculty development, however: the apathy of administrators, the resistance of faculty, excessive expenditures of time and money, lack of the faculty's involvement in the design of the evaluation scheme, and lack of consistent feedback to the faculty (Arreola 1983; Miller 1974; Moomaw 1977a).

Post-tenure review should have a direct link to faculty development and should not operate in isolation from faculty development practices.

The coupling of evaluation with development is not a novel concept. When it works effectively, the cycle is one in which "evaluation data will reveal areas in need of improvement; improvement of these areas will yield better instruction; better instruction will stimulate improved student learning" (Prodgers 1980). Apart from improvement, however, tenured faculty have other personal and professional needs that post-tenure evaluation, in tandem with faculty development, should address. Institutions must provide "systematic attention to refreshing . . . existing faculty" (Smith 1978, p. 15) and, "to maintain vitality among professors, . . . must offer new opportunities for growth and renewal" (Baldwin 1982, p. 1). "Individual development may be primary to, or of equal importance with, institutional goals. . . . That is, unless faculty get in touch with themselves they will not relate effectively to students" (Martin 1975, p. 195).[3] Thus, faculty development becomes:

> *. . . an institutional process [that] seeks to modify the attitudes, skills, and behavior of faculty members toward greater competence and effectiveness in meeting student*

3. See also Bergquist and Phillips 1975; Brookes and German 1983; Gaff and Justice 1978; Gross 1977; Hammons 1983; Kanter 1979; Martin 1975; Neff 1976; Nelsen and Siegel 1980; Novotny 1981; Seldin 1981; Smith 1976, 1983; and Wergin, Mason, and Munson 1976 for more information about faculty development activities.

needs, their own needs, and the needs of the institution (Francis 1973, p. 72).

Generally, three broad categories of activities constitute what has come to be classified as faculty development. First are those activities whose purpose is instructional improvement—instructional evaluation, diagnosis with videotape, microteaching, or workshops on curriculum development and the like. Second are activities like team building and management development that purport to improve the organizational climate. Third are personal development activities through which faculty growth is fostered—counseling, career planning workshops, and training in interpersonal skills (Bergquist and Phillips 1975).

In the past, most institutions emphasized the first category of activities—those designed to improve teaching (Gaff and Justice 1978; Seldin 1981). A recent study, however, indicates that many institutions are now broadening this emphasis to include faculty members' personal lives (McMillen 1985).

Although one survey of faculty development practices in colleges and universities in the United States showed that 60 percent of the institutions responding had a program or set of practices on their campuses, the findings also showed "poor participation [in these activities] among faculty needing improvement" (Centra 1976, p. 60).

How to involve faculty in such activities, short of coercion, is a nagging concern. One possible answer is to weave faculty development activities into the evaluation of the faculty (Centra 1976). And growth contracts are a possible means of achieving that task (Centra 1976; Smith 1976).

Growth contracts. Similar in many respects to management by objectives, the concept embodied in growth contracts has as its core the belief that individual goals and institutional goals can be aligned so as to promote faculty growth and institutional accomplishment (Pfnister et al. 1979). In operation, this concept transforms into a process whereby an individual faculty member and the dean or department chair establish a plan of work (including professional development activities and goals as appropriate), methods of accomplishing work goals, the criteria against which the faculty member will be evaluated, the timeline for accomplishing the goals, and needed institutional resources (Baldwin 1982; Centra 1976; Eble 1973; Seldin 1977).[4] The system has several advantages: the faculty member's advance knowledge of how he or she will be evaluated and the ability to supply input to the process, a faculty plan of work that includes assignments revolving around the faculty member's strengths and development activities designed to help any deficiencies, and the assurance that feedback will occur to develop the subsequent individual growth contract (Seldin 1980, p. 7).

Whether growth contracts are viable for all types of institutions is not clear at this time. Their use at the community college level is increasing (Centra 1976), but more "objection than support" is apparent at research-oriented universities (Pfnister et al. 1979, p. 38). The reason for such objection may be based in part on some institutions' rejection of their incompatibility with the five assumptions necessary for implementing a growth contract:

1. *Individual members of a department have different talents, expertise, and potential for contributing to the effectiveness of a department and to the college or university as a whole. . . .*
2. *The effectiveness of the department (institutional unit) can be maintained (enhanced/improved) if the talents of individual members can be emphasized and diversity of assignments maintained. . . .*
3. *In a period of limited and often decreasing fiscal resources, under the threat of retrenchment, departments can more effectively meet the challenge of more systematic planning for college and institutional needs. . . .*
4. *The reward system within the department/institution can be adjusted to take into account differential assignments, and such an adjustment should be made. . . .*

4. Institutions that have used growth contracts include Gordon College (Massachusetts), Coe College (Iowa), New College of the University of Alabama, College of the Mainland (Texas), Wharton County Junior College (Texas), Ottawa University (Kansas), Las Medaras College (California), Medical College of Virginia, Columbus College (Georgia), and Austin College (Texas) (Smith 1976).

5. *The faculty growth contract can be applied to all disciplines and all academic units . . .* (Pfnister et al. 1979, pp. 33–38).

Growth contracts may be a useful and beneficial strategy for implementing the outcomes of post-tenure evaluation in institutions that can accept these assumptions and are committed "to experiment, invest resources, accept criticism, and risk failure in order to stimulate genuine professional development" (Baldwin and Blackburn 1981, p. 608).

Guiding Principles for Administrative Procedures

In addition to the commonly held and respected principles of evaluation that may be helpful to institutions involved in the investigation, development, modification, or revision of a post-tenure evaluation system, certain procedural principles must also be considered.

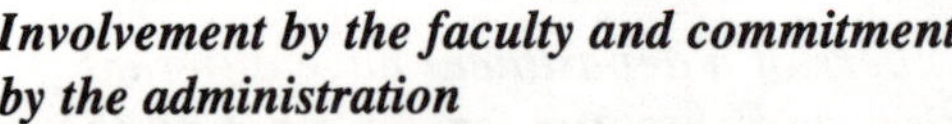

Involvement by the faculty and commitment by the administration

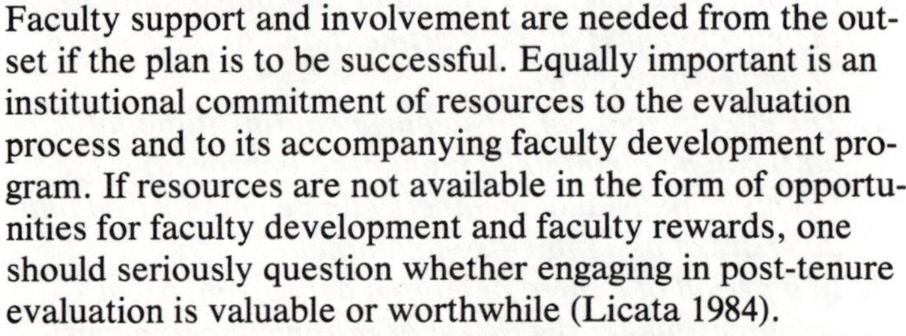

Faculty support and involvement are needed from the outset if the plan is to be successful. Equally important is an institutional commitment of resources to the evaluation process and to its accompanying faculty development program. If resources are not available in the form of opportunities for faculty development and faculty rewards, one should seriously question whether engaging in post-tenure evaluation is valuable or worthwhile (Licata 1984).

Other guidelines apply specifically to the post-tenure review process:

- *Use faculty peers, not administrators, to evaluate.*
- *[E]nsure that the review panel is not [comprised] of the same persons who review professors for tenure and promotion.*
- *Conduct the reviews every three to five years, but certainly not annually.*
- *Rely on multiple sources of information, especially in regard to teaching, including evaluation by peers, students, and alumni.*
- *Offer the faculty member responsibility for collecting the information to be included in a file for evaluation.*

Base evaluation only on the contents of the file (Heller 1985a, p. 29).

Institutional consensus on the aftermath of a substandard post-tenure review

What options does an institution have when all efforts—either a growth contract or other developmental strategies—do not result in identified improvement? What actions can an institution take when a faculty member refuses to act upon the recommendations emanating from the evaluation?

Institutions must grapple with and resolve to some extent these two gnawing issues before forging down the post-tenure evaluation road. Unfortunately, the literature almost totally ignores treatment of such issues.

In institutions where post-tenure review is adopted for the purpose of reaffirming or reevaluating the original award of tenure, the dilemma becomes also one of combating possible censure by the AAUP, avoiding an outcry from the faculty, and ultimately constructing a case of dismissal for cause that can be upheld in the courts—no easy task for even the best of institutions. Most supporters of post-tenure evaluation do not endorse a summative direction, however, because it tends to disenfranchise the tenure doctrine. Instead, what receives sanction is a formative process that peacefully coexists with tenure. At issue, though, is the question of whether peaceful coexistence can endure if no action or progress results. Under such a circumstance, what actions should follow from the institution? Apart from disallowing merit awards or pay increases, refusing to approve sabbaticals, and denying promotions, the only other practice that warrants some attention is encouraging or counseling faculty into early retirement or a career change (Bagshaw 1985; Patton 1983). An estimated 200-plus institutions have some form of early retirement or career change program in place, which generally takes the form of a liberalized actuarial reduction, lump-sum severance payments, annuity enhancements, phased retirement, retraining for outplacement, paid retraining, and supplemental earnings (Patton 1983). The scope of such plans, however, depends to a large degree on the individual institution and is "relatively meaningless if they are developed in isolation from a larger plan for institutional vitality'' (p. 54).

Clearly, the other remaining option is to take no action and to keep trying to effect change through developmental tactics, an issue that faculty and institutional leaders must address before the unfolding of periodic review. If no action is taken as a result of the evaluation when faculty can definitely see a need for some action, ''reviews will be discredited and regarded as a waste of time in addition to an intrusive action'' (Moses 1985, p. 39). Reviews need to be detailed in such a way so that some action can follow. Outstanding faculty must receive visible rewards, and areas for new development must be established for those faculty who need fresh endeavors and reset targets, with available institutional assistance for nonperforming faculty. If nonperformers persist to be nonperformers, some institutional action seems unavoidable.

If properly developed with extensive faculty involvement in design and carefully put into operation with an appropriate commitment of institutional resources, post-tenure evaluation may have the potential to offer an opportunity for renewal, revitalization, and quality assurance. Simultaneously, post-tenure review is not to be endorsed haphazardly or necessarily by all institutions. If improperly orchestrated, it can be pernicious, divisive, and threatening to institutional health.

The context in which an institution operates and its nature must be considered carefully before post-tenure evaluation is developed. Some institutions may wish to thoughtfully consider the reasons why post-tenure review tends to be topical on their campuses. Certain campuses may then choose to develop alternative and more satisfactory ways for themselves to deal with the problems that post-tenure evaluation purports to address, such as early retirement incentives or arrangements for career changes. Still other institutions may have positive evidence that the numerous evaluations they conduct before granting salary increments, promotions, sabbaticals, and so on are quite effective in maintaining a high level of quality, vitality, and renewal among the faculty.

CONCLUSIONS AND IMPLICATIONS

Institutional leaders face multiple challenges over the next decade. Predictions are that extrinsic forces will pressure campus decision makers into developing mechanisms to enhance faculty vitality and renew institutional quality and viability. The increasing numbers of tenured faculty, the continual graying of the professoriate, the persistent career immobility of faculty, and the apparent pervasive erosion of job satisfaction within higher education have prompted some in the field to call for an examination of faculty evaluation and development practices after the award of tenure.

Interest in the concept and process of post-tenure evaluation is growing. While some scholars and practitioners are highly skeptical about the idea of formal, periodic review of faculty, others in the field see value in such a process, particularly if it is formative in nature and directly linked to opportunities for faculty development and faculty rewards. Support for a summative post-tenure evaluation system that primarily serves to remove tenured faculty for cause is far less compelling and usually endorsed only by outside publics, boards of trustees, or governing bodies.

Support for a summative post-tenure evaluation system that primarily serves to remove tenured faculty for cause is far less compelling.

Based on what is known about faculty evaluation in general and from some limited research studies specifically dealing with post-tenure evaluation, the following recommendations are made for institutions interested in developing or modifying a plan to evaluate tenured faculty:

1. *The purpose for the evaluation should drive all other aspects of the evaluation plan.* Institutions must decide whether the evaluation will be formative or summative in nature. Once decided, the purpose should be clearly articulated to the college community, as the purpose will affect who evaluates faculty and the frequency of evaluation. Formative evaluations, for example, generally occur less frequently than summative evaluations; three- or five-year intervals are most frequently noted.
2. *Faculty must be involved in the design of the plan.* Experience has shown that any evaluation system needs administrative commitment and faculty involvement if it is to be successful.
3. *Faculty and administrators should agree upon the specifics of the plan.* Extrapolating from pretenure evaluation models can be helpful. In particular, the

post-tenure evaluation plan should include multiple sources of input, identified areas and criteria to be assessed, and agreed-upon assessment standards.

4. *The need for flexibility and individualization in a post-tenure evaluation plan should not be overlooked.* Institutions must take a more singular perspective when establishing professional work objectives, for as faculty age and mature, their interests and priorities change accordingly. Formative post-tenure evaluation schemes must recognize this fact and respond supportively to such transitions.
5. *Faculty development programs should be linked to a post-tenure evaluation system.* If institutional commitment to faculty development and provision for faculty rewards cannot be delivered, then institutions should seriously question the usefulness and effectiveness of such evaluation (Licata 1984). Institutions must also have resolved what actions are appropriate if no improvement occurs after a substandard evaluation.
6. *Innovative approaches to post-tenure evaluation and institutional planning are needed.* The concept of a faculty growth contract deserves renewed attention because of what it can contribute to the process of aligning institutional needs with faculty interests.

Whether the recent surge of national attention on the topic of evaluation of tenured faculty persists remains to be seen. Whether institutions embrace the concept of post-tenure evaluation as a means of self-regulation and renewal also remains to be seen. What is evident is the glaring need for more research on the status of post-tenure evaluation, the practices employed by different institutions, and the effectiveness of such institutional practices in accomplishing their stated purpose, which can be helpful to institutions embarking on an examination of the issue. This monograph is a first attempt at broadening the research base.

The present and projected age and tenure profile of higher education faculty entreats institutional leaders to find ways to nourish the professional lives of the faculty at their institutions. One should not underplay the reservations expressed regarding the unnecessary paperwork and the potential destructiveness to collegial relationships, academic freedom, and the rigor of pretenure review that this process might cause. Therein lies the threat.

Nevertheless, the constructive benefits that a formative system might also provide should not be automatically discounted. In the end, individual institutions must decide whether such a process is viable. The determination should be based on a careful assessment of the institution's need, readiness, and potential for successful implementation, and of the anticipated positive and negative ramifications.

Institutions have much invested in their tenured faculty. For some institutions, post-tenure evaluation tied to faculty development may be but one way to protect and renew a critical human resource—the resource that directly helps shape institutional flexibility and quality. And therein lies the opportunity.

APPENDIX A

SURVEY OF THE STATUS OF POST-TENURE EVALUATION

Representatives from 43 institutions participated in an ACE Leadership Development Program on Periodic Review of Tenured Faculty in November 1984. They were subsequently surveyed to determine the status of post-tenure evaluation at their institutions. Of the 30 responding institutions, 16 indicated the existence of a formal plan on their campuses (a list of those institutions is at the end of this appendix), and another eight indicated that their institutions were in the process of developing a formal system. Two institutions indicated interest emerging on the horizon.

Purpose

The primary reported purpose of the evaluation plan was summative in the case of seven institutions; that is, the results of the evaluation were used to make personnel decisions related to promotion, salary, and retention. In two institutions, the evaluation served as a mechanism for determining merit pay, and in four institutions, the purpose was solely formative and tied to individual faculty development. Three institutions combined formative and summative purposes.

Effectiveness

Six institutions said the evaluation was effective in accomplishing its stated purpose, eight indicated an uncertainty about the effectiveness, and two indicated the plan to be ineffective.

Frequency

At eight institutions, the evaluation is conducted annually. In the remaining eight institutions, faculty are evaluated at intervals of two to five years.

Participants

Individuals involved in the evaluation included the dean only (four cases); the department chair only (three cases); the dean and the chair (three cases); the dean, the chair, and a committee of peers (four cases); and the dean, the chair, a committee of peers, and students (two cases).

Process Followed

At most of the institutions, the tenured faculty member prepares some form of a self-evaluation, updated curriculum vitae, or activity analysis sheet. At 10 institutions, the department chair (or dean) meets with the faculty member to discuss the year's accomplishments, after which the faculty member is evaluated. In five of those 10 institutions, student evaluations are reviewed as part of the process. Six institutions use evaluations by a committee of peers as well as the department chair's review and student evaluations.

Institutions Reporting a Post-tenure Evaluation Process

1. Bergen Community College, Parasmus, New Jersey
2. Berry College, Mount Berry, Georgia
3. Eastern Michigan University, Ypsilanti, Michigan
4. Incarnate Word College, San Antonio, Texas
5. Manhattanville College, Purchase, New York
6. New York City Technical College, Brooklyn, New York
7. Northern Kentucky University, Highland Heights, Kentucky
8. Oakton Community College, Des Plaines, Illinois
9. Simmons College, Boston, Massachusetts
10. Simpson College, Indianola, Iowa
11. Texas Tech University, Lubbock, Texas
12. University of Missouri–Rolla, Rolla, Missouri
13. University of North Florida, Jacksonville, Florida
14. University of Texas at Dallas, Richardson, Texas
15. University of Wisconsin–Stevens Point, Stevens Point, Wisconsin
16. Utah State University, Logan, Utah

APPENDIX B

SOURCES OF SAMPLE RATING FORMS FOR FACULTY EVALUATION

Peer/Colleague Evaluation Forms

1. Braskamp, L. A., et al. 1983. *Guidebook for Evaluating Teaching*. Urbana: University of Illinois, Office of Instructional Resources, Measurement and Research Division; and Beverly Hills, Cal.: Sage. Form # reproduced in Seldin, Peter. 1984. *Changing Practices in Faculty Evaluation*. San Francisco: Jossey-Bass.
   - Peer Evaluation of Teaching Materials Form, p. 162

2. French-Lazovik, Grace. 1981. "Peer Review: Documentary Evidence in the Evaluation of Teaching." In *Handbook of Teacher Evaluation,* edited by J. Millman. Beverly Hills, Cal.: Sage. Form reproduced in Whitman, Neal, and Weiss, Elaine. 1982. *Faculty Evaluation: The Use of Explicit Criteria for Promotion, Retention, and Tenure*. AAHE-ERIC Higher Education Research Report No. 2. Washington, D.C.: American Association for Higher Education.
   - Suggested Format for Peer Review of Undergraduate Teaching Based on Dossier Materials, pp. 36–38

3. Hoyt, Donald P. 1982. "Using Colleagues' Ratings to Evaluate the Faculty Member's Contribution to Instruction." In *Practices That Improve Teaching Evaluation,* edited by G. French-Lazovik. New Directions for Teaching and Learning No. 11. San Francisco: Jossey-Bass.
   - Sample Form for Collecting Faculty Observations of Colleagues' Indirect Contributions to Instructional Programs, p. 69

4. Miller, Richard. 1972. *Evaluating Faculty Performance*. San Francisco: Jossey-Bass.
   - Classroom Visitation Appraisal Form, p. 33
   - Teaching Materials and Procedures Appraisal Form, p. 34
   - Faculty Service and Relations Appraisal Form, p. 47
   - Professional Status and Activities Appraisal Form, p. 55
   - Book Appraisal Form, p. 58
   - Monograph Appraisal Form, p. 59
   - Special Book Appraisal Form, p. 60
   - Chapter in a Book Appraisal Form, p. 61
   - Periodical/Article Appraisal Form, p. 62
   - Public Service Appraisal Form, p. 67

5. Seldin, Peter. 1984. *Changing Practices in Faculty Evaluation*. San Francisco: Jossey-Bass.

- Report of Classroom Observation Report, p. 163
- Report of Classroom Observation Report, p. 165
- Peer Self-Appraisal of Faculty Service, p. 174
- Peer Appraisal of Research/Publication Work, p. 175
- Peer Evaluation of Research Activity, p. 176

6. Wilson, R. C., and Dienst, E. R. 1971. *Users' Manual: Teacher Description Questionnaires*. Berkeley, Cal.: Center for Research and Development in Higher Education. Reproduced in Miller, R. 1974. *Developing Programs for Faculty Evaluation*. San Francisco: Jossey-Bass.
   - Colleague Description of Teachers, Short Form, pp. 22–23
   - Colleague Description of Teachers, Medium Length Form, pp. 24–25

Self-Evaluation Forms

1. Centra, John A. 1979. *Determining Faculty Effectiveness*. San Francisco: Jossey-Bass.
   - Form for Faculty Self-Evaluation, p. 52
   - Self-Appraisal Form for Faculty (developed by San Jose State University 1976), p. 53

2. Miller, Richard I. 1972. *Evaluating Faculty Performance*. San Francisco: Jossey-Bass.
   - Self-Appraisal of Teaching, p. 37
   - Research—Self-Evaluation, p. 71

3. Seldin, Peter. 1980. *Successful Faculty Evaluation Programs*. New York: Coventry Press.
   - Faculty Self-Evaluation Report, pp. 92–93
   - Faculty Activity Report, p. 94

4. Seldin, Peter. 1984. *Changing Practices in Faculty Evaluation*. San Francisco: Jossey-Bass. From Braskamp, L. A., et al. 1983. *Guidebook for Evaluating Teaching*. Urbana: University of Illinois, Office of Instructional Resources, Measurement and Research Division; and Beverly Hills, Cal.: Sage.
   - Instructor Self-Evaluation on Teaching, pp. 171–73
   - Instructor Self-Evaluation Report on Teaching, pp. 167–70

Student Evaluation Forms

1. Center for Faculty Evaluation and Development. 1981. Instructional Development and Effectiveness Assessment (IDEA) Form. Manhattan: Kansas State University.

2. Centra, John A. 1979. *Determining Faculty Effectiveness*. San Francisco: Jossey-Bass.
   - Colorado State University Academic Advising Review Form, p. 128
   - Ohio State University Annual Student Evaluation of College Advising, p. 13

3. Miller, Richard I. 1972. *Evaluating Faculty Performance*. San Francisco: Jossey-Bass.
   - Student Appraisal of Teaching, p. 28
   - Student Appraisal of Advising, p. 45

4. Miller, Richard I. 1974. *Developing Programs for Faculty Evaluation*. San Francisco: Jossey-Bass.
   - Student Instructional Report, pp. 37–42
   - Student Description of Teaching—Short Form, pp. 43–44
   - Student Description of Teaching—Long Form, pp. 45–48
   - The Purdue Rating Scale for Instruction, pp. 51–55
   - Course Evaluation, pp. 53–54
   - Survey of Student Opinion of Teaching, pp. 55–56
   - Course Evaluation Questionnaire, pp. 57–59

5. Seldin, Peter. 1980. *Successful Faculty Evaluation Programs*. New York: Coventry Press.
   - Student Perceptions of Learning and Teaching, pp. 50–53
   - Sample Questionnaire for Classroom, pp. 53–56
   - Student Appraisal of Advising, pp. 112–13
   - Student Appraisal of Advising, pp. 114–15
   - Advising Survey Form, pp. 116–18

REFERENCES

The ERIC Clearinghouse on Higher Education abstracts and indexes the current literature on higher education for the Office of Educational Research and Improvement's monthly bibliographic journal, *Resources in Education.* Most of these publications are available through the ERIC Document Reproduction Service (EDRS). For publications cited in this bibliography that are available from EDRS, ordering number and price are included. Readers who wish to order a publication should write to the ERIC Document Reproduction Service, 3900 Wheeler Avenue, Alexandria, Virginia, 22304. When ordering, please specify the document number. Documents are available as noted in microfiche (MF) and paper copy (PC). Because prices are subject to change, it is advisable to check the latest issue of *Resources in Education* for current cost based on the number of pages in the publication.

Books and Periodicals

Aleomoni, Lawrence M. 1984. "The Dynamics of Faculty Evaluation." In *Changing Practices in Faculty Evaluation,* written and edited by Peter Seldin. San Francisco: Jossey-Bass.

Allhouse, Merle F. 1974. "Tenure? A Quest for Truth and Freedom." *Soundings* 57: 471–81.

American Association of University Professors. 1979. "Academic Freedom and Tenure." *AAUP Bulletin* 56: 25–29.

———. 1982. "Recommended Institutional Regulations and Academic Freedom and Tenure." In *AAUP Policy Documents and Reports*. Washington, D.C.: AAUP.

———. November/December 1983. "On Periodic Evaluation of Tenured Faculty." *Academe* 69: 1a–14a.

———. 1984a. *Policy Documents and Reports*. Washington, D.C.: AAUP. ED 260 623. 191 pp. MF–$0.97; PC–$16.97.

———. September/October 1984b. "Report of Committee A." *Academe* 70: 24a.

AAUP/AAC Commission on Academic Tenure. 1973. *Faculty Tenure: A Report and Recommendations*. San Francisco: Jossey-Bass.

Andrews, Hans. 1985. *Evaluating for Excellence*. Stillwater, Okla.: New Forum Press.

Arreola, Raoul A. 1983. "Establishing a Successful Faculty Evaluation and Development Program." In *Evaluating Faculty and Staff,* edited by A. Smith. New Directions for Community Colleges No. 41. San Francisco: Jossey-Bass.

Arreola, Raoul A., and Heinrich, D. 1977. "A Model for Differential Norming of Faculty Evaluations for Promotion and Tenure Decisions." Paper presented at the annual meeting of the American Educational Research Association, April 4–8, New York, New York. ED 146 227. 56 pp. MF–$0.97; PC–$7.14.

Astin, Alexander W., and Lee, C. B. T. 1967. "Current Practices in the Evaluation and Training of College Teachers." In *Improving College Teaching,* edited by C. B. Lee. Washington, D.C.: American Council on Education.

Aubrecht, Judith D. 1984. "Better Faculty Evaluation Systems." In *Changing Practices in Faculty Evaluation,* written and edited by Peter Seldin. San Francisco: Jossey-Bass.

Austin, Ann, and Gamson, Z. F. 1983. *Academic Workplace: New Demands, Heightened Tensions.* ASHE-ERIC Higher Education Research Report No. 10. Washington, D.C.: Association for the Study of Higher Education. ED 243 397. 131 pp. MF–$0.97; PC–$12.96.

Ayers, Claude V. 1979. "The Effects of Voiding the Tenure Policy at Surry Community College." Unpublished practicum thesis, Nova University. ED 199 691. 18 pp. MF–$0.97; PC–$3.54.

Bagshaw, Marque. 1985. "Managing Resource Uncertainty through Academic Staffing in Four-Year Colleges and Universities." Paper presented at the annual meeting of the Association for the Study of Higher Education, 16 March, Chicago, Illinois.

Bailey, Stephen K. 1974. "The Effective Use of Human Resources." In *The Effective Use of Resources: Financial and Human.* Washington, D.C.: Association of Governing Boards. ED 096 913. 33 pp. MF–$0.95; PC–$5.34.

Baldridge, J. Victor, and Kemerer, F. R. 1981. *Assessing the Impact of Faculty Collective Bargaining.* AAHE-ERIC Higher Education Research Report No. 8. Washington, D.C.: American Association for Higher Education. ED 216 653. 66 pp. MF–$0.97; PC–$7.10.

Baldwin, Roger G. 1979. "Adult Career Development: What Are the Implications for Faculty?" *Current Issues in Higher Education* No. 2. Washington, D.C.: American Association for Higher Education. ED 193 998. 44 pp. MF–$0.97; PC not available EDRS.

———. 1982. "Fostering Faculty Vitality: Options for Institutions and Administrators." *Administrator's Update.* Washington, D.C.: American Association of University Administrators/ERIC. ED 220 069. 8 pp. MF–$0.97; PC–$3.54.

Baldwin, Roger G., and Blackburn, R. T. 1981. "The Academic Career as a Developmental Process: Implications for Higher Education." *Journal of Higher Education* 52: 598–614.

Baldwin, Roger G.; Brakeman, Louis; Edgerton, Russell; Hagberg, Janet; and Mahar Thomas. 1981. *Expanding Faculty Options: Career Development Projects at Colleges and Universities.* Washington, D.C.: American Association for Higher Education. ED 217 780. 114 pp. MF–$0.97; PC–$11.16.

Batista, Enrique E. 1976. "The Place of Colleague Evaluation in the Appraisal of College Teaching: A Review of the Literature." *Research in Higher Education* 4: 257–71.

Bayer, A. E., and Dutton, J. E. 1977. "Career Age and Research—Professional Activities of Academic Scientists: Tests of Alternative Nonlinear Models and Some Implications for Higher Education Faculty Policies." *Journal of Higher Education* 48: 259–82.

Bennett, John B. 1985. "Periodic Evaluation of Tenured Faculty Performance." In *Leadership and Institutional Renewal,* edited by R. A. Davis. New Directions for Higher Education No. 49. San Francisco: Jossey-Bass.

Bennett, John B., and Chater, S. S. Spring 1984. "Evaluating the Performance of Tenured Faculty Members." *Educational Record* 65: 38–41.

Benton, Sidney E. 1982. *Rating College Teaching: Criterion Studies of Student Evaluation-of-Instruction Instruments.* AAHE-ERIC Higher Education Research Report No. 1. Washington, D.C.: American Association for Higher Education. ED 221 147. 57 pp. MF–$0.97; PC–$7.14.

Bergquist, William H., and Phillips, S. R. 1975. "Components of an Effective Faculty Development Program." *Journal of Higher Education* 46: 177–211.

Bevan, John M. 1980. "Faculty Evaluation and Institutional Rewards." *AAHE Bulletin* 33 (12): 1–15.

———. 1982. "The Chairman: Product of Socialization or Learning." In *Practices That Improve Teaching Evaluation,* edited by G. French-Lazovik. New Directions for Teaching and Learning No. 11. San Francisco: Jossey-Bass.

Blackburn, Robert T. 1972. *Tenure: Aspects of Job Security on the Changing Campus.* Atlanta: Southern Regional Education Board. ED 068 005. 65 pp. MF–$0.97; PC–$7.14.

Blackburn, Robert T., and Clark, M. F. 1975. "An Assessment of Faculty Performance: Some Correlates between Administrator, Colleague, Student, and Self-Ratings." *Sociology of Education* 48(2): 242–56.

Bolden, Samuel H. 1979. "Current Status, Policy, and Criteria for the Evaluation of Tenured Faculty in Alabama's Four-year Public Institutions of Higher Education." Ed.D. dissertation, Auburn University.

Boyd, James E., and Schietinger, E. G. 1976. *Faculty Evaluation Procedures in Southern Colleges and Universities.* Atlanta: Southern Regional Education Board. ED 121 153. 54 pp. MF–$0.97; PC–$7.14.

Braskamp, Larry A., et al. 1983. *Guidebook for Evaluating Teaching.* Urbana: University of Illinois, Office of Instructional

Resources, Measurement and Research Division; and Beverly Hills, Cal.: Sage.

Braskamp, Larry A.; Fowler, D. L.; and Ory, J. C. 1984. "Faculty Development and Achievement: A Faculty's View." *Review of Higher Education* 7: 205–22.

Brewster, Kingman, Jr. 1972. "On Tenure." *AAUP Bulletin* 58: 381–83.

Brookes, Michael C. T., and German, K. L. 1983. *Meeting the Challenges: Developing Faculty Careers*. ASHE-ERIC Higher Education Research Report No. 3. Washington, D.C.: Association for the Study of Higher Education. ED 232 516. 54 pp. MF–$0.97; PC–$7.14.

Brown, R. S., Jr. 1976. "Financial Exigency." *AAUP Bulletin* 62(1): 5–16.

Burson, Gerald E. 1982. "A Concern for Professionalism." Unpublished paper. ED 221 237. 13 pp. MF–$0.97; PC–$3.54.

Carnegie Council on Policy Studies in Higher Education. 1980. *Three Thousand Futures: The Next Twenty Years for Higher Education*. San Francisco: Jossey-Bass.

Carnegie Foundation for the Advancement of Teaching. 1985. "The Faculty: Deeply Troubled." *Change* 17: 31–34.

Carr, Robert K. Spring 1972. "The Uneasy Future of Academic Tenure." *Educational Record* 53: 119–27.

Cartter, Alan M., ed. 1975. *Assuring Academic Progress without Growth*. San Francisco: Jossey-Bass.

Case, Chester H. 1971. "The Quality Control Model of Evaluation and the Development Model for Faculty Growth and Evaluation." Unpublished paper. ED 047 669. 16 pp. MF–$0.97; PC–$3.54.

Centra, John A. 1972. *Two Studies on the Utility of Student Ratings for Instructional Improvement*. Princeton, N.J.: Educational Testing Service.

———. 1975. "Colleagues as Raters of Classroom Instruction." *Journal of Higher Education* 46: 327–38.

———. 1976. *Faculty Development Practices in United States Colleges and Universities*. Princeton, N.J.: Educational Testing Service. ED 141 382. 96 pp. MF–$0.97; PC–$9.36.

———. 1978. "Types of Faculty Development Programs." *Journal of Higher Education* 49: 151–62.

———. 1979. *Determining Faculty Effectiveness*. San Francisco: Jossey-Bass.

Chait, Richard P. 1979. "Tenure and the Academic Future." In *Tenure, Three Views,* edited by J. O'Toole, W. W. Van Alstyne, and R. P. Chait. New Rochelle, N.Y.: Change Magazine Press.

———. 1980. "Setting Tenure and Personnel Policies." In *Handbook of College and University Trusteeship,* edited by Richard T. Ingram and associates. San Francisco: Jossey-Bass.

Chait, Richard, and Ford, A. T. 1982. *Beyond Traditional Tenure*. San Francisco: Jossey-Bass.

Chickering, Arthur W. 1984. "Faculty Evaluation: Problems and Solutions." In *Changing Practices in Faculty Education,* edited by P. Seldin. San Francisco: Jossey-Bass.

Cohen, Arthur M. Summer 1974. "Evaluation of Faculty." *Community College Review* 11: 2–22.

Cohen, Arthur M., and Brawer, F. B. 1969. *Measuring Faculty Performance*. Washington, D.C.: American Association of Junior Colleges. ED 031 222. 90 pp. MF–$0.97; PC–$9.36.

———. 1982. *The American Community College*. San Francisco: Jossey-Bass.

Cohen, Peter A. 1980. "Effectiveness of Student-Rating Feedback for Improving Instruction: A Meta-Analysis of Findings." *Research in Higher Education* 13: 321–41.

———. 1981. "Student Ratings of Instruction and Student Achievement: A Meta-Analysis of Multisection Validity Studies." *Review of Educational Research* 51: 281–301.

———. 1983. "Comment on a Selective Review of the Validity of Student Ratings of Teaching." *Journal of Higher Education* 54: 448–58.

Cohen, Peter A., and McKeachie, W. J. 1980. "The Role of Colleagues in the Evaluation of College Teaching." *Improving College and University Teaching* 28(4): 147–54.

Corwin, Thomas M. 1978. "A Research Perspective on Mandatory Retirement." In *Changing Retirement Policies*. Current Issues in Higher Education No. 4. Washington, D.C.: American Association for Higher Education. ED 193 991. 31 pp. MF–$0.97; PC not available EDRS.

Corwin, T. M., and Knepper, P. R. 1978. *Finance and Employment Implications of Raising the Mandatory Retirement Age for Faculty*. Policy Analysis Service Reports 4 (1). Washington, D.C.: American Council on Education. ED 163 868. 72 pp. MF–$0.97; PC–$7.14.

Costin, Frank; Greenough, W.; and Menges, R. 1971. "Student Ratings of College Teaching: Reliability, Validity, and Usefulness." *Review of Educational Research* 41: 511–35.

Cox, Charles. September 1973. "Tenure on Trial in Virginia." *Change* 5: 11–14.

Creswell, John W. 1985. *Faculty Research Performance: Lessons from the Sciences and the Social Sciences*. ASHE-ERIC Higher Education Report No. 4. Washington, D.C.: Association for the Study of Higher Education.

Cyert, Richard. 1980. "The Management of Universities of Constant or Decreasing Size." In *Strategies for Retrenchment: National, State, Institutional.* Current Issues in Higher Education No. 6. Washington, D.C.: American Association for Higher Education. ED 194 009. 48 pp. MF–$0.97; PC not available EDRS.

Davidson, James F. Spring 1982. "Tenure, Governance, and Standards in the American Community." *Liberal Education* 68: 35–46.

Di Biase, Elaine. 1980. "Tenure, Alternatives to Tenure, and the Courts." Paper presented to the American Educational Research Association, April 7–11, Boston, Massachusetts. ED 185 696. 32 pp. MF–$0.97; PC–$5.34.

Dowell, D. A., and Neal, J. P. 1982. "A Selective Review of the Validity of Student Ratings of Teaching." *Journal of Higher Education* 52: 51–62.

Dressel, Paul L. 1976. *Handbook of Academic Evaluation.* San Francisco: Jossey-Bass.

Eble, Kenneth E. 26 April 1971. "Teaching: Despite Attacks on Tenure, There Is No Evidence That It Actually Leads to Ineffective Teaching." *Chronicle of Higher Education:* 8.

———. 1973. "Tenure and Teaching." In *The Tenure Debate,* edited by B. L. Smith. San Francisco: Jossey-Bass.

———. 1982. "Can Faculty Objectively Evaluate Teaching?" In *Practices That Improve Teaching Evaluation,* edited by G. French-Lazovik. New Directions for Teaching and Learning No. 11. San Francisco: Jossey-Bass.

———. 1984. "New Directions in Faculty Evaluation." In *Changing Practices in Faculty Evaluation,* edited by P. Seldin. San Francisco: Jossey-Bass.

Eddy, Margot S. 1981. "Faculty Response to Retrenchment." *AAHE-ERIC Research Currents.* Washington, D.C.: American Association for Higher Education. ED 202 446. 5 pp. MF–$0.97; PC–$3.54.

Edwards, Scott. 1974. "A Modest Proposal for the Evaluation of Teaching." *Liberal Education* 60: 316–26.

Erickson, Glenn R., and Erickson, B. L. 1974. "Improving College Teaching: An Evaluation of a Teaching Consultation Procedure." *Journal of Higher Education* 50: 670–83.

Erikson, Erik H. 1978. *Adulthood.* New York: W. W. Norton & Co.

Faculty Affairs Committee, Earlham College. 2 May 1975. "Assessment and Development of Tenured Faculty." Memo to the faculty.

Farrell, Charles S. 8 December 1982. "They Took My Chair Away: Effects of Layoffs on Tenured Faculty." *Chronicle of Higher Education:* 23–25.

Feldman, Kenneth A. 1976. "The Superior College Teacher from the Students' View." *Research in Higher Education* 5: 253–65.

Francis, John S. 1973. "How Do We Get There from Here?" In *Facilitating Faculty Development,* edited by M. Freedman. New Directions in Higher Education No. 1. San Francisco: Jossey-Bass.

French-Lazovik, Grace. 1981. "Peer Review: Documentary Evidence in the Evaluation of Teaching." In *Handbook of Teacher Evaluation,* edited by J. Millman. Beverly Hills, Cal.: Sage.

Friedman, Stephen. 15 May 1984. "Merit Pay: The Ultimate Insult to Teachers." *Chronicle of Higher Education:* 32.

Furniss, W. Todd. 1978. *Responding with Quality: The Closing System of Academic Employment*. Atlanta: Southern Regional Education Board. ED 160 032. 82 pp. MF–$0.97; PC–$9.36.

———. 1981. *Reshaping Faculty Careers*. Washington, D.C.: American Council on Education.

Gaff, Jerry G., and Justice, D. O. 1978. "Faculty Development Yesterday, Today, and Tomorrow." In *Institutional Revival through the Improvement of Teaching,* edited by J. Gaff. New Directions for Higher Education No. 24. San Francisco: Jossey-Bass.

Galm, John A. Spring 1985. "Welcome to Post-tenure Review." *College Teaching* 33: 65–67.

Geis, George L. 1984. "The Context of Evaluation." In *Changing Practices in Faculty Evaluation,* edited by P. Seldin. San Francisco: Jossey-Bass.

George, Linda K., and Winfield-Laird, I. 1984. "Implications of an Aging Faculty for the Quality of Higher Education and Academic Careers." In *Teaching and Aging,* edited by Chandra N. Mehrotra. New Directions for Teaching and Learning No. 19. San Francisco: Jossey-Bass.

Gillmore, Gerald. 1983–84. "Student Ratings as a Factor in Employment Decisions and Periodic Review." *Journal of College and University Law* 10: 557–76.

Gould, Roger L. 1978. *Transformations: Growth and Change in Adult Life*. New York: Simon & Schuster.

Greene, Robert T. 1976. "The Impact of the Commonwealth of Virginia's State-Supported Colleges and Universities Academic Tenure and Faculty Activity Study." Paper presented at a meeting of the American Council on Education, Washington, D.C. ED 132 926. 42 pp. MF–$0.97; PC–$5.34.

Greenwood, Gordon E., and Ramagli, H. J., Jr. 1980. "Alternatives to Student Ratings of College Teaching." *Journal of Higher Education* 51: 673–84.

Gross, Alan. 1977. "Twilight in Academe: The Problem of the Aging Professoriate." *Phi Delta Kappan* 58: 752–54.

Gustad, J. W. 1961. *Policies and Practices in Faculty Evaluation.* Washington, D.C.: American Council on Education, Committee on College Teaching.

Habecker, Eugene B. 1981. "A Systematic Approach to the Study of Benefits and Detriments of Tenure in American Higher Education: An Analysis of the Evidence." Unpublished paper. ED 212 208. 66 pp. MF–$0.97; PC–$7.14.

Hall, D. T., and Nougaim, K. 1968. "An Examination of Maslow's Need Hierarchy in an Organizational Setting." *Organizational Behavior and Human Performance* 3: 12–35.

Hammons, James. 1983. "Faculty Development: A Necessary Corollary to Faculty Evaluation." In *Evaluating Faculty and Staff,* edited by A. Smith. New Directions for Community Colleges No. 41. San Francisco: Jossey-Bass.

Heim, Peggy. 1978. "Implications of Mandatory Retirement Legislation for Institutions of Higher Education." In *Changing Retirement Policies*. Current Issues in Higher Education No. 4. Washington, D.C.: American Association for Higher Education. ED 193 991. 31 pp. MF–$0.97; PC not available EDRS.

Heller, Scott. 19 September 1984a. "Two Years after Laying Off 58 Faculty Members, Temple University Still Feels the Aftershocks." *Chronicle of Higher Education:* 23+.

———. 21 November 1984b. "Growing Pains at Texas Tech: Faculty and President Clash over Tenure." *Chronicle of Higher Education:* 19–22.

———. 16 January 1985a. "Review of Tenured Professors Will Not Work if It's Viewed as a Threat, Administrators Say." *Chronicle of Higher Education:* 29–31.

———. 16 January 1985b. "Union Contracts Said to Permit Faculty Review." *Chronicle of Higher Education:* 30.

Hellweg, Susan A., and Churchman, D. A. Fall 1981. "The Academic Era of Retrenchment." *Planning for Higher Education* 10: 16–18.

Hendrickson, Robert M., and Lee, B. A. 1983. *Academic Employment and Retrenchment: Judicial Review and Administrative Action*. ASHE-ERIC Higher Education Research Report No. 8. Washington, D.C.: Association for the Study of Higher Education. ED 240 972. 133 pp. MF–$0.97; PC–$12.96.

Higher Education and National Affairs. 11 November 1985. "Bennett Calls for System to Assess Higher Education" 34: 6.

Hind, Robert R.; Dornbusch, S.; and Scott, W. P. 1974. "A Theory of Evaluation Applied to a University Faculty." *Sociology of Education* 47 (1): 114–28.

Hodgkinson, Harold L. 1974. "Adult Development: Implications for Faculty and Administrators." *Educational Record* 55: 263–74.

Irby, D. M. 1978. "Clinical Faculty Development." In *Clinical Education for the Health Professions,* edited by C. Ford. St. Louis: C. V. Mosby & Co.

Kanter, Rosabeth Moss. 1979. "Changing the Shape of Work: Reform in Academe." In *Perspectives on Leadership*. Current Issues in Higher Education No. 2. Washington, D.C.: American Association for Higher Education. ED 193 997. 26 pp. MF–$0.97; PC not available EDRS.

Kaplan, William. 1978. *The Law of Higher Education*. San Francisco: Jossey-Bass.

Kearl, Bryant. November/December 1983. "Remarks." *Academe* 69: 8a–10a.

Kerr, Clark. 1980. "Basic Point: 1980." *Association of Governing Boards Reports* 22 (2): 3–13.

Kirschling, Wayne R. 1978. "Evaluating Faculty Performance and Vitality." In New Directions for Institutional Research No. 20. San Francisco: Jossey-Bass.

Kleingartner, Archie. 1984. "Post-tenure Evaluation and Collective Bargaining." Paper presented at the American Council on Education Conference, Periodic Review of Tenured Faculty, November, Miami, Florida.

Kronk, Annie K., and Shipka, T. A. 1980. *Evaluation of Faculty in Higher Education*. Washington, D.C.: National Education Association.

Kulik, J. A. 1974. "Evaluation of Teaching." Memo to the faculty 54. Ann Arbor: University of Michigan, Center for Research on Learning and Teaching. ED 092 025. 6 pp. MF–$0.97; PC–$3.54.

Kurland, Jordan E. November/December 1983. "On Periodic Evaluation of Tenured Faculty." *Academe* 69: 1a–14a.

Landini, Richard G. November/December 1983. "Remarks." *Academe* 69: 11a–12a.

Lang, Theodore H. 1975. "Teacher Tenure as a Management Problem." *Phi Delta Kappan* 56: 459–62.

Larsen, Charles M. November/December 1983. "Remarks." *Academe* 69: 10a–11a.

Lawrence, Janet. 1984. "Faculty Age and Teaching." In *Teaching and Aging,* edited by C. M. N. Mehrotra. New Directions for Teaching and Learning No. 19. San Francisco: Jossey-Bass.

Lee, Barbara A. 1985. "Commentary. Raising the Hurdle: Judicial Reaction to Heightened Standards for Promotion and Tenure." *West's Education Law Reporter* 20: 357–64.

Levinson, Daniel J. 1978. *The Seasons of a Man's Life*. New York: Ballantine.

Lewis, Lionel S. 1975. *Scaling the Ivory Tower*. Baltimore: Johns Hopkins University Press.

———. 18 July 1984. "Trying to Define 'Merit' in Academe." *Chronicle of Higher Education:* 56.

Licata, Christine M. 1984. "An Investigation of the Status of Post-tenure Evaluation in Selected Community Colleges in the United States." Ed.D. dissertation, The George Washington University.

Linnell, Robert H. 1979. "Age, Sex, and Ethnic Trade-Offs in Faculty Employment: You Can't Have Your Cake and Eat It Too." In *Employment Practices in Academe*. Current Issues in Higher Education No. 4. Washington, D.C.: American Association for Higher Education. ED 194 000. 21 pp. MF–$0.97; PC not available EDRS.

Linney, Thomas. 1979. "Alternatives to Tenure." *AAHE-ERIC Higher Education Research Currents*. Washington, D.C.: American Association for Higher Education. ED 165 694. 6 pp. MF–$0.97; PC–$3.54.

Lombardi, John. Winter 1974. "Community Colleges—When Facilities are Reduced." *Change* 6: 55–56.

McCurdy, Jack. 12 December 1984. "California State University Faculty Members to Vote on Pact Giving Them 10 Percent Raise, Control over Merit Pay." *Chronicle of Higher Education:* 21.

McKeachie, Wilbert J. 1983. "Faculty as a Renewable Resource." In *College Faculty: Versatile Human Resources in a Period of Constraint,* edited by Roger G. Baldwin and Robert T. Blackburn. New Directions for Institutional Research No. 40. San Francisco: Jossey-Bass.

McKeachie, Wilbert J., and Lin, Y. G. 1975. *Use of Student Ratings in Evaluation of College Teaching*. Ann Arbor: University of Michigan. ED 104 284. 41 pp. MF–$0.97; PC–$5.34.

McMillen, Liz. 28 November 1984. "A Handful of 2-Year Colleges Awarding 'Merit' Raises to Outstanding Teachers." *Chronicle of Higher Education:* 27+.

———. 13 November 1985. "Many Faculty-Development Programs Add New Dimension: Professors' Personal Lives." *Chronicle of Higher Education:* 27+.

Mark, Sandra F. 1977. *Faculty Evaluation Systems: A Research Study of Selected Community Colleges in New York State*. New York: State University of New York, Faculty Council of

Community Colleges. ED 158 809. 152 pp. MF–$0.97; PC–$11.57.

Marquis, Todd E.; Lane, D. M.; and Dorfman, P. 1979. "Is There a Consensus Regarding What Constitutes Effective Teaching?" *Journal of Educational Psychology* 71: 840–49.

Marsh, Herbert W. 1982. "Validity of Students' Evaluations of College Teaching: A Multitrait-Multimethod Analysis." *Journal of Educational Psychology* 74: 264–79.

Marsh, Herbert W., and Overall, J. U. 1980. "Validity of Students' Evaluations of Teaching Effectiveness: Cognitive and Affective Criteria." *Journal of Educational Psychology* 72: 468–75.

———. 1982. "Students' Evaluations of Teaching: An Update." *AAHE-ERIC Research Currents*. Washington, D.C.: American Association for Higher Education. ED 225 473. 5 pp. MF–$0.97; PC–$3.54.

Martin, Warren B. May 1975. "Faculty Development as Human Development." *Liberal Education* 61: 187–96.

Melchiori, Gerlinda S. 1982. *Planning for Program Discontinuance: From Default to Design*. AAHE-ERIC Higher Education Research Report No. 5. Washington, D.C.: American Association for Higher Education.

Menges, Robert. 1979. "Evaluating Teaching Effectiveness: What Is the Proper Role for Students?" *Liberal Education* 65: 356–70.

Metzger, Walter P. 1979. "The History of Tenure." *AAHE Current Issues in Higher Education* No. 6. Washington, D.C.: American Association for Higher Education. ED 194 002. 21 pp. MF–$0.97; PC not available EDRS.

Miller, Keith R. 30 April 1979. "Tenure: A Cause of Intellectual Cowardice?" *Chronicle of Higher Education:* 72.

Miller, Richard I. 1972. *Evaluating Faculty Performance*. San Francisco: Jossey-Bass.

———. 1974. *Developing Programs for Faculty Evaluation*. San Francisco: Jossey-Bass.

Mingle, James, and associates. 1981. *The Challenges of Retrenchment*. San Francisco: Jossey-Bass.

Mix, Marjorie C. 1978. *Tenure and Termination in Financial Exigency*. AAHE-ERIC Higher Education Research Report No. 3. Washington, D.C.: American Association for Higher Education. ED 152 222. 37 pp. MF–$0.97; PC–$5.34.

Montana Commission on Postsecondary Education. 1974. "Revised Recommendation: Commission on Postsecondary Education." ED 095 736. 54 pp. MF–$0.97; PC–$7.14.

Moomaw, W. Edward. 1977a. *Faculty Evaluation for Improved Learning*. Atlanta: Southern Regional Education Board. ED 149 683. 66 pp. MF–$0.97; PC–$7.14.

———. 1977b. "Practices and Problems in Evaluating Instruction." In *Renewing and Evaluating Teaching,* edited by J. A. Centra. New Directions for Higher Education No. 17. San Francisco: Jossey-Bass.

Moore, Kathryn M. 1980. "Academic Tenure in the United States." *Journal of the College and University Personnel Association* 31 (3–4): 1–17.

Mortimer, Kenneth P.; Bagshaw, Marque; and Masland, Andrew T. 1985. *Flexibility in Academic Staffing: Effective Policies and Practices*. ASHE-ERIC Higher Education Report No. 1. Washington, D.C.: Association for the Study of Higher Education. ED 260 675. 121 pp. MF–$0.97; PC–$11.16.

Mortimer, Kenneth P., and Tierney, Michael L. 1979. *The Three "R's" of the Eighties: Reduction, Retrenchment, and Reallocation*. AAHE-ERIC Higher Education Research Report No. 4. Washington, D.C.: American Association for Higher Education. ED 172 642. 78 pp. MF–$0.97; PC–$9.36.

Moses, Ingrid. 1985. "What Academics Think about Regular Reviews of Performance." *Australian Universities' Review* 28(1): 34–40.

Myers, Betty J., and Pearson, R. E. 1984. "Personal Perspectives of Academic Professionals Approaching Retirement." In *Teaching and Aging,* edited by Chandra M. Mehrotra. New Directions for Teaching and Learning No. 19. San Francisco: Jossey-Bass.

National Center for Education Statistics. 1983. "Number of Full-time Instructional Faculty on 9- and 12-month Contracts in Institutional Units of Higher Education by Level, 1981–82." Unpublished raw data.

National Commission on Higher Education Issues. 1982. *To Strengthen Quality in Higher Education*. Washington, D.C.: American Council on Education. ED 226 646. 20 pp. MF–$0.97; PC–$3.54.

Neff, Charles B. 1976. "Faculty Development Tug O'War, Or Up a Tree with a Tuning Fork." *Liberal Education* 62: 427–31.

Nelsen, William C., and Siegel, M. E. 1980. "Faculty Development: Promises, Realities, and Needs." In *Effective Approaches to Faculty Development,* edited by W. C. Nelsen and M. E. Siegel. Washington, D.C.: Association of American Colleges. ED 184 439. 154 pp. MF–$0.97; PC–$15.17.

Nisbet, Robert. April 1973. "The Future of Tenure." *Change* 5: 27–33.

Novotny, Janet L. 1981. "Mandatory Retirement of Higher Education Faculty." *AAHE-ERIC Research Currents*. Washington, D.C.: American Association for Higher Education. ED 197 693. 6 pp. MF–$0.97; PC–$3.54.

O'Connell, William R., Jr., and Smartt, S. H. 1979. *Improving Faculty Evaluation: A Trial in Strategy*. Atlanta: Southern Regional Education Board. ED 180 395. 43 pp. MF–$0.97; PC–$5.34.

Olswang, Steven G. 1982–83. "Planning the Unthinkable: Issues in Institutional Reorganization and Faculty Reductions." *Journal of College and University Law* 9: 431–49.

Olswang, Steven G., and Fantel, J. I. 1980–81. "Tenure and Periodic Performance Review: Compatible Legal and Administrative Principles." *Journal of College and University Law* 7: 1–30.

Olswang, Steven G., and Lee, B. A. 1984. *Faculty Freedoms and Institutional Accountability: Interactions and Conflicts*. ASHE-ERIC Higher Education Research Report No. 5. Washington, D.C.: Association for the Study of Higher Education. ED 252 170. 90 pp. MF–$0.97; PC–$9.36.

Orpen, Christopher. Spring 1982. "Tenure and Academic Productivity: Another Look." *Improving College and University Teaching* 30: 60–62.

Ory, John C., and Braskamp, Larry A. 1981. "Faculty Perceptions of the Quality and Usefulness of Three Types of Evaluative Information." *Research in Higher Education* 15: 271–82.

O'Toole, James. 1978. "Tenure: A Conscientious Objection." *Change* 10 (6): 24–31.

Patton, Carl U. 1983. "Institutional Practices and Faculty Who Leave." In *College Faculty: Versatile Human Resources in a Period of Constraint,* edited by R. G. Baldwin and R. T. Blackburn. New Directions for Institutional Research No. 40. San Francisco: Jossey-Bass.

Perry, Suzanne. 21 September 1983. "Formal Reviews for Tenured Professors: Useful Spur or Orwellian Mistake?" *Chronicle of Higher Education:* 25–27.

Pfnister, Allan, et al. 1979. "Growth Contracts: Viable Strategy for Institutional Planning under Changing Conditions?" In *Faculty Career Development*. Current Issues in Higher Education No. 2. Washington, D.C.: American Association for Higher Education. ED 193 998. 44 pp. MF–$0.97; PC not available EDRS.

Prodgers, Stephen. January 1980. "Toward Systematic Faculty Evaluation." *Regional Spotlight* 13. Atlanta: Southern Regional Education Board. ED 181 833. 9 pp. MF–$0.97; PC–$3.54.

Riley, Bob F. 1980. "Faculty Tenure in Community Colleges of Texas: Where It Came From—Where It Is Going." Unpublished manuscript. ED 192 845. 26 pp. MF–$0.97; PC–$5.34.

Roemer, Robert E., and Schnitz, J. E. 1982. "Academic Employment as Day Labor: The Dual Labor Market in Higher Education." *Journal of Higher Education* 53: 514–31.

Rose, Clare. 1976. "Faculty Evaluation in an Accountable World: How Do You Do It?" Paper presented to the national conference of the American Association for Higher Education, March, Chicago, Illinois. ED 144 442. 17 pp. MF–$0.97; PC–$3.54.

Rotem, Arie. 1978. "The Effects of Feedback from Students to University Instructors." *Research in Higher Education* 9: 308–18.

Roueche, John. 1984. "Merit Pay: The University of Texas Model." Presentation at the National Conference on Merit Pay, October, Columbia, Maryland.

St. Thomas, Sister, and Kennedy, M. P. 1980. "An Analysis of the Tenure System at Norwich University and Implications for Change." Unpublished practicum, Nova University. ED 212 315. 47 pp. MF–$0.97; PC–$5.34.

Schulman, Benson R., and Trudell, J. W. 1972. "California's Guidelines for Teacher Evaluation." *Community and Junior College Journal* 43 (2): 32–34.

Schuster, Jack H., and Bowen, Howard R. September/October 1985. "The Faculty at Risk." *Change* 17: 12–21.

Scully, Malcolm G. 8 December 1982. "Colleges, States Weigh Rules to Make Tenure Harder to Get, Easier to Lose." *Chronicle of Higher Education:* 1+.

———. 26 October 1983. "4,000 Faculty Members Laid Off in 5 Years by 4-Year Institutions, Survey Shows." *Chronicle of Higher Education:* 21.

Seldin, Peter. 1977. *Faculty Growth Contracts*. London, England: University of London, Institute of Education. ED 157 469. 17 pp. MF–$0.97; PC–$3.54.

———. 1980. *Successful Faculty Evaluation Programs*. New York: Coventry Press.

———. 1981. "Faculty Development Programs." *Exchange* 6: 17–21.

———. 1982. "Self-Assessment of College Teaching." *Improving College and University Teaching* 30 (2): 70–74.

———. 1984. *Changing Practices in Faculty Evaluation*. San Francisco: Jossey-Bass.

Shapiro, Harold T. November/December 1983. "The Privilege and the Responsibility." *Academe* 69: 3a–7a.

Sheehy, Gail. 1976. *Passages: Predictable Crises in Adult Life*. New York: Bantam Books.

Shulman, Carol H. 1979. *Old Expectations, New Realities: The Academic Profession Revisited*. AAHE-ERIC Higher Education Research Report No. 2. Washington, D.C.: American Association for Higher Education. ED 169 874. 58 pp. MF–$0.97; PC–$7.14.

Silber, John R. 1973. "Tenure in Context." In *The Tenure Debate,* edited by B. Smith. San Francisco: Jossey-Bass.

Smith, Albert B. 1976. *Faculty Development and Evaluation in Higher Education*. AAHE-ERIC Higher Education Research Report No. 8. Washington, D.C.: American Association for Higher Education. ED 132 891. 85 pp. MF–$0.97; PC–$9.36.

———. 1983. "A Conceptual Framework for Staff Evaluation." In *Evaluating Faculty and Staff,* edited by A. Smith. New Directions for Community Colleges No. 41. San Francisco: Jossey-Bass.

Smith, Bardwell L. 1974. "The Problem Is Not Tenure." *Soundings* 57: 458–70.

Smith, Donald K. 1978. "Faculty Vitality and the Management of University Personnel Policies." In *Evaluating Faculty Performance and Vitality,* edited by W. R. Kirschling. New Directions for Institutional Research No. 20. San Francisco: Jossey-Bass.

Smith, Sylvia. 1984. "Case Study of Merit Pay at Brookdale Community College." Presentation at the National Conference on Merit Pay, October, Columbia, Maryland.

Southern Regional Education Board. 1977. *Faculty Evaluation for Improved Learning*. Atlanta: SREB. ED 149 683. 66 pp. MF–$0.97; PC–$7.14.

Stern, Carol S. November/December 1983. "Remarks." *Academe* 69: 12a–13a.

Super, D. E. 1980. "A Life-Span, Life-Space Approach to Career Development." *Journal of Vocational Behavior* 16: 282–98.

Trow, Martin. 1977. *Aspects of American Higher Education 1969–1975: A Report for the Carnegie Council on Policy Studies in Higher Education*. ED 134 085. 40 pp. MF–$0.97; PC not available EDRS.

Tucker, Allan, and Mautz, R. Spring 1982. "Academic Freedom, Tenure, and Incompetence." *Educational Record* 62: 22–25.

University of Utah Commission to Study Tenure. 1971. Final Report. Salt Lake City: Author. ED 052 747. 186 pp. MF–$0.97; PC–$16.97.

Van Alstyne, William W. 1978. "Tenure: A Conscientious Objection." *Change* 10(9): 44–47.

Walden, Theodore. Fall 1979. "Tenure and Academic Productivity." *Improving College and University Teaching* 27: 154–57.

———. 1980. "Tenure: A Review of the Issues." *Educational Forum* 44: 363–72.

Wergin, Jon F.; Mason, E. J.; and Munson, P. J. 1976. "The Practice of Faculty Development." *Journal of Higher Education* 47: 289–308.

Whitman, Neal, and Weiss, E. 1982. *Faculty Evaluation: The Use of Explicit Criteria for Promotion, Retention, and Tenure.* AAHE-ERIC Higher Education Research Report No. 2. Washington, D.C.: American Association for Higher Education. ED 221 148. 57 pp. MF–$0.97; PC–$10.80.

Zaharis, John L. 1973. "Developing Guidelines for Faculty Reduction in a Multicampus College." Unpublished manuscript. ED 087 508. 51 pp. MF–$0.97; PC–$7.14.

Zuckert, Michael P., and Friedhoff, J. Spring 1980. "Reviewing Tenured Faculty." *Improving College and University Teaching* 28: 50.

Court Cases

AAUP v. *Bloomfield College,* 136 N.J. Super. 249, 346 A.2d 615 (1975).

Bignall v. *North Idaho College,* 538 F.2d 243 (9th Cir. 1976).

Board of Regents v. *Roth,* 408 U.S. 564 (1972).

Brenna v. *Southern Colorado State College,* 589 F.2d 475 (10th Cir. 1978).

Browzin v. *Catholic University of America,* 527 F.2d 843 (D.C. Cir. 1975).

Johnson v. *Board of Regents of the University of Wisconsin System,* 377 F. Supp. 227 (W.D. Wisc. 1974), *aff'd,* 510 F.2d 975 (7th Cir. 1975).

Klein v. *the Board of Higher Education of the City of New York,* 434 F. Supp. 1113 (S.D.N.Y. 1977).

Krotkoff v. *Goucher College,* 585 F.2d 675 (4th Cir. 1978).

Levitt v. *Board of Trustees of Nebraska State College,* 376 F. Supp. 945 (D. Neb. 1974).

Lumpert v. *University of Dubuque,* 225 N.W. 2d 168 (Iowa Ct. of Appeals 1977).

Scheuer v. *Creighton University,* 260 N.W. 2d 595 (1977).

INDEX

P

ASHE-ERIC HIGHER EDUCATION REPORTS

Starting in 1983, the Association for the Study of Higher Education assumed cosponsorship of the Higher Education Reports with the ERIC Clearinghouse on Higher Education. For the previous 11 years, ERIC and the American Association for Higher Education prepared and published the reports.

Each report is the definitive analysis of a tough higher education problem, based on a thorough research of pertinent literature and institutional experiences. Report topics, identified by a national survey, are written by noted practitioners and scholars with prepublication manuscript reviews by experts.

Eight monographs (10 monographs before 1985) in the ASHE-ERIC Higher Education Report series are published each year, available individually or by subscription. Subscription to eight issues is $60 regular; $50 for members of AERA, AAHE and AIR: $40 for members of ASHE. (Add $7.50 outside the United States.)

Prices for single copies, including 4th class postage and handling, are $10.00 regular and $7.50 for members of AERA, AAHE, AIR, and ASHE ($7.50 regular and $6.00 for members for 1983 and 1984 reports, $6.50 regular and $5.00 for members for reports published before 1983). If faster 1st class postage is desired for U.S. and Canadian orders, add $.75 for each publication ordered: overseas, add $4.50. For VISA and MasterCard payments, include card number, expiration date, and signature. Orders under $25 must be prepaid. Bulk discounts are available on orders of 15 or more reports (not applicable to subscriptions). Order from the Publications Department, Association for the Study of Higher Education, One Dupont Circle, Suite 630, Washington, D.C. 20036, 202/296-2597. Write for a publication list of all the Higher Education Reports available.

1986 Higher Education Reports

1. Post-tenure Faculty Evaluation: Threat or Opportunity?
   Christine M. Licata

1985 Higher Education Reports

1. Flexibility in Academic Staffing: Effective Policies and Practices
   Kenneth P. Mortimer, Marque Bagshaw, and Andrew T. Masland
2. Associations in Action: The Washington, D.C., Higher Education Community
   Harland G. Bloland
3. And on the Seventh Day: Faculty Consulting and Supplemental Income
   Carol M. Boyer and Darrell R. Lewis
4. Faculty Research Performance: Lessons from the Sciences and Social Sciences
   John W. Creswell
5. Academic Program Reviews: Institutional Approaches, Expectations, and Controversies
   Clifton F. Conrad and Richard F. Wilson
6. Students in Urban Settings: Achieving the Baccalaureate Degree
   Richard C. Richardson, Jr., and Louis W. Bender

7. Serving More Than Students: A Critical Need for College Student Personnel Services
   Peter H. Garland
8. Faculty Participation in Decision Making: Necessity or Luxury?
   Carol E. Floyd

1984 Higher Education Reports

1. Adult Learning: State Policies and Institutional Practices
   K. Patricia Cross and Anne-Marie McCartan
2. Student Stress: Effects and Solutions
   Neal A. Whitman, David C. Spendlove, and Claire H. Clark
3. Part-time Faculty: Higher Education at a Crossroads
   Judith M. Gappa
4. Sex Discrimination Law in Higher Education: The Lessons of the Past Decade
   J. Ralph Lindgren, Patti T. Ota, Perry A. Zirkel, and Nan Van Gieson
5. Faculty Freedoms and Institutional Accountability: Interactions and Conflicts
   Steven G. Olswang and Barbara A. Lee
6. The High-Technology Connection: Academic Industrial Cooperation for Economic Growth
   Lynn G. Johnson
7. Employee Educational Programs: Implications for Industry and Higher Education
   Suzanne W. Morse
8. Academic Libraries: The Changing Knowledge Centers of Colleges and Universities
   Barbara B. Moran
9. Futures Research and the Strategic Planning Process: Implications for Higher Education
   James L. Morrison, William L. Renfro, and Wayne I. Boucher
10. Faculty Workload: Research, Theory, and Interpretation
    Harold E. Yuker

1983 Higher Education Reports

1. The Path to Excellence: Quality Assurance in Higher Education
   Laurence R. Marcus, Anita O. Leone, and Edward D. Goldberg
2. Faculty Recruitment, Retention, and Fair Employment: Obligations and Opportunities
   John S. Waggaman
3. Meeting the Challenges: Developing Faculty Careers
   Michael C. T. Brookes and Katherine L. German
4. Raising Academic Standards: A Guide to Learning Improvement
   Ruth Talbott Keimig

5. Serving Learners at a Distance: A Guide to Program Practices
   Charles E. Feasley
6. Competence, Admissions, and Articulation: Returning to the Basics in Higher Education
   Jean L. Preer
7. Public Service in Higher Education: Practices and Priorities
   Patricia H. Crosson
8. Academic Employment and Retrenchment: Judicial Review and Administrative Action
   Robert M. Hendrickson and Barbara A. Lee
9. Burnout: The New Academic Disease
   Winifred Albizu Meléndez and Rafael M. de Guzmán
10. Academic Workplace: New Demands, Heightened Tensions
    Ann E. Austin and Zelda F. Gamson

NOTES

RANDALL LIBRARY-UNCW
3 0490 0037422 Y